Deco Serging

April L. Dunn

First U.S. edition published in 1997
©1997 April L. Dunn

Publishers Cataloging in Publication Data
Dunn, April L.
DecoSerging:
Decorative Serging Techniques
1. Sewing, Machine   2. Serging   I. Title
Library of Congress Catalog Card Number:
96-084264

ISBN# 0-9641201-2-7
1 0   9   8   7   6   5   4   3   2   1
Printed in the United States of America

The information in this book is presented in
good faith, but no warranty is given nor results
guaranteed. Dragon Threads and April Dunn assume
no responsibility for the use of this information.

Dragon Threads
410 Canyon Drive North
Columbus, Ohio 43214

Editor: Linda Chang Teufel
Book Design & Illustrations:
Kimberly Radomsky, Diana Jung
Associate Editor: Raymond Foeller
Photography: Larry Friar

Dedication

To my husband Mike, and son Ryan,
who fended for themselves too many times to count,
while I taught, sewed, or wrote.

To the memory of my father, Allan Gilpin,
and grandmother Geraldine Gilpin,
who both watch over me.

And of course my mother, Emma Gilpin,
who gave me so much of
who I am and my love for fabrics.

Table of Contents

Acknowledgments

My book, like all others, could not have been possible without the contributions of many people to whom I would like to give credit here.

I want to thank Linda Teufel who, when I came to her with this book idea, was as excited as I was. She showed lots of patience and tolerance during the writing of this book for my many family trials and tribulations, not to mention three moves.

Special thanks go to Kim Radomsky for the book design; Diana Jung for Photogallery design, book layout and illustrations; and Larry Friar for the photographs. Without these three people, my words would be pretty boring. Also thanks to Ray Foeller for editing my words and grammar.

A special thanks to Amy Dukes Smith, who over ten years ago said yes. This started my direct involvement within the home sewing industry. She also introduced me to Fred and Lorraine Westberry of Tampa, Florida, who allowed me the use of their classroom space and let me develop my teaching talents.

J.P. Burke and Associates, Pamela and Jack, who have become such good friends, both professional and personal. Thanks for *ThreadPRO* and *Stitch and Ditch,* not only are they wonderful products, but without them, we would never have met.

I want to give thanks to the following sewing friends who have tested and helped proofread this book many times: Jean Bohman, Judy Foster, Donna Hoeflinger, Jenny Osborn, Ellen Sorensen and Sandy Troutman.

A warm thanks to the people at ELNA Inc. and ELNA USA for the use of a sewing machine, a press and sergers used in the photo shoot and to make samples. I especially want to thank Jane Burbach, Paula Spoon and Chris Tryon for their assistance.

I want to thank the following sewing machine companies for the loan of a serger and accessories for the photo shoot and to construct samples: Baby Lock, Bernina of America, Brother International Corporation, New Home Sewing Machine Company, Juki Industries of America, Pfaff American Sales Corporation, Riccar, Singer Sewing Company, Husqvarna Viking and White Sewing Machine Company.

There are many other companies who contributed items used in this book for samples and photographs:

• American and Efird for *Signature* and *Maxi-Lock* threads.

• YLI Corporation, Lanny and Vicki Smith, for *Candlelight, Jeans Stitch, Woolly Nylon, Monét, Designer 6, Success, Pearl Crown Rayon, Wonder Invisible* thread, *Spark Organdy,* silk ribbon, and acrylic and metallic embroidery threads.

• Madeira (A division of SCS USA) and Ed Moore, for *Glamour, Decor 6, Super Twist,* rayon and metallic threads, *Jewel* hologram thread, *Monofil* and metallic and embroidery needles.

• Sulky of America and Fred Drexler, for rayon and metallic embroidery thread, *Sliver* and stabilizers.

• June Tailor for cutting mats and the *Heirloom Stitcher's Shape 'n Press* pressing/pinning board.

• Fiskars for a rotary cutter and ruler.

• Sullivans for *Metafil* needles, rayon and metallic machine embroidery threads and *Fray Stop.*

• Darr Inc. for the *EZ Winder*

Thanks to many sewing machine dealers, guilds and sewing organizations around the U.S., Canada and Italy who invited and encouraged me to teach and try new things.

Last, but certainly not least, thanks to my many students around the world who have guided me towards this project, as much as I guided them through their projects.

Introduction

As I set out to write this book on texturizing and decorative serging techniques, I realized that just like my students, my readers are at all different levels in their serging life and familiarity with their machines. Therefore, the book is arranged into three general sections. These sections start with the basics and continue on with decorative information and novelty techniques.

Understanding the Basics can be used as an introduction to serging, a refresher course or a reference section. Here are sections about your machine, its parts, and information to help you become familiar with the general, or generic, terminology used throughout the book. You will also find illustrations and descriptions of what the different types of tension set-ups should look like. You may need to refer to these for the techniques. *Basics* also includes sections that contain an examination of decorative serging. It covers many different types of decorative threads, problem solving and many helpful tips to make your serging more successful. I have even included stitch reference charts which you can customize to your machine's settings for future reference.

Fabric Techniques is devoted to a variety of applications for innovative and decorative serging techniques. These techniques use all different types of stitches in conjunction with decorative threads to achieve many different effects. They use fabric, ribbon, charms and more to result in a newly created piece of fabric.

The book concludes with the *Trims*. These sections put the final touch on DecoSerging just as the trims put the final creative touch to your own projects.

I hope you use this book to learn more about your serger and discover what a fun and creative machine it can be!

HAPPY SERGING!

Understanding The Basics

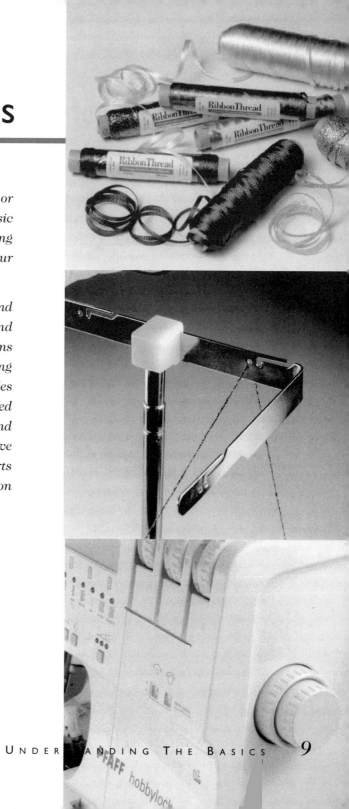

These sections are provided so anyone with a serger, at any skill or knowledge level can use this book. By providing you with basic serger operation/terminology, as well as decorative serging information, you have a reference, or refresher, course right at your finger tips.

The first sections cover general information and terminology about your serger. You will find descriptions and illustrations for what tensions should "LOOK" like for reference during techniques. The last few sections in Basics includes information about decorative serging. Included here are helpful hints and a description and reference chart for the most popular decorative threads. Personal DecoSerging Tension Charts have been included for you to complete, based on your serger settings.

The Parts of Your Serger

There are many parts of your serger and although it is important to be familiar with them all, the parts which are most important to the general understanding of serger operation are highlighted here. Understanding the basics of your machine will help you become more comfortable with it for everyday use as well as for DecoSerging.

You may wish to sit in front of your serger with this book and your operating manual to identify each of these parts. Although your manual may have a different name for various parts, the terms I use are general/generic ones.

CUTTING SYSTEMS

Sergers are designed to trim away excess fabric as part of the whole serging process. There are two different kinds of cutting systems found on sergers: the hanging blade system and the recessed system. Each system consists of two parts: the fixed or (stationary) cutter and the movable cutter.

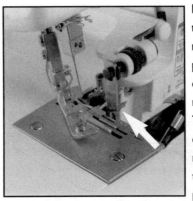

Hanging blade system- One part of the cutting system hangs from a working mechanism that is to the right of the presser foot and shank. As the serger operates you can see the movable blade move in an up and down cutting motion. The movable blade hangs almost in front of the right overlock needle. This machine has a raised, curved portion in the door that protects you and your project from the working mechanism.

Recessed cutting system- In this system the movable blade is less exposed. It is set into a recessed portion of the presser foot and plate. It is shaped like a question mark and is found "down" under the serging area.

Both systems cut efficiently but the movable cutting blades work in an opposite manner on the two systems. In the recessed system, when the blade is set to cut, it is up; but when the hanging blade is set to cut, the blade is down. For this reason, when referring to the cutter position for a technique, the terms "cutting/non-cutting", or "engaged/disengaged" will be used instead of up or down.

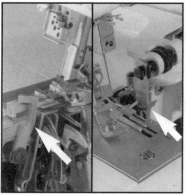

Movable cutter/blade- This is the part of the cutting system that moves when the machine runs or the hand wheel is turned. It can hang from the top, or it can look like a question mark and come from under the plate. It can be viewed more easily when the front door is open.

Stationary or fixed cutter/blade- This is the straight, flat part of the cutter system. It appears to be a cut out portion of the plate and is found under the presser foot. The movable blade presses against the fixed cutter. This portion of the cutting system does not move when the serger is running, hence the name. It is viewed more easily when the presser foot is lifted up or removed. On most sergers this can be adjusted to help determine how much fabric is cut off, for a smooth end result. How and where to adjust the fixed cutter varies with different models. On some sergers it is described as the width adjustment (see discussion under plate/stitch finger). If you have any questions about where to find, or how to make this adjustment, consult your owner's manual or local dealer.

STITCH LENGTH

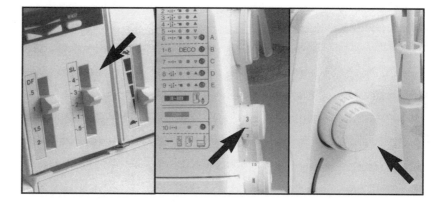

This serger setting determines the distance between each stitch formation or how close the stitches are to each other. The lower the setting, the closer the stitches are to each other; the higher the setting, the farther apart the stitches form. Normal stitch length for most machines is 2.0-3.0.

The location of the control may be found in a variety of places on different machines (the front; the right side/above the hand wheel; inside the front door; inside the left/side door) and may require a screwdriver to adjust. If you have any questions about where to find this adjustment, consult your owner's manual.

PLATE/STITCH FINGER

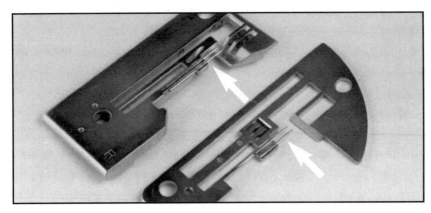

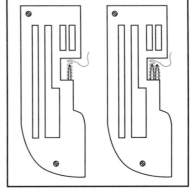

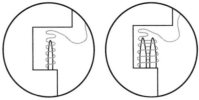

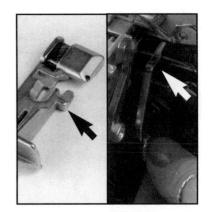

All sergers have a needle plate (as do all sewing machines). Some sergers come with extra plates and others have extra plates available as optional accessories. The plate is mentioned here because it is the part that determines the true width of the stitch formation. Some sergers have a width adjustment dial, but this dial usually adjusts the fixed cutter position (discussed earlier) and determines how much fabric is left to "stuff" into the serged edge. There is only a slight effect to the width unless you are sewing with multiple layers of fabric and/or the fabric is very stiff. There are a few sergers where the "width" adjustment actually moves the stitch finger and the fixed cutter at the same time.

The loopers form the stitch over a portion of the plate (and/or foot) called the stitch finger.

Some sergers have a stitch finger in the presser foot, some are detachable, some swing out of the way, and some "width" adjustment knobs move finger positions. The stitch finger determines the stitch width... narrow stitch fingers for narrow stitches, wide stitch fingers (or a combination of stitch fingers) for wider stitches.

NEEDLE POSITIONS AND NEEDLES

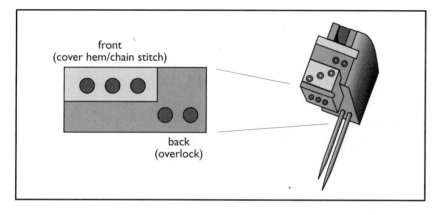

front
(cover hem/chain stitch)

back
(overlock)

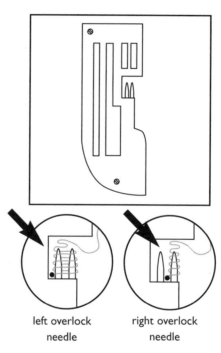

left overlock
needle

right overlock
needle

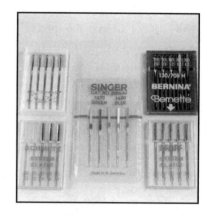

In traditional 4-thread sergers, the two needles do essentially the same thing, but in different positions. The needles are side by side, like a twin needle, and lock the thread loops, formed by the loopers over the stitch fingers, together and onto the fabric.

With 5-thread sergers, the left and right (or front and back) needle positions do different types of stitches. The right (back) positions are for 2-thread, the 3-thread and 4-thread overlocking/overcasting, while the left (front) needle position(s) is for chain stitching and possibly a cover hem stitch. Some 5-thread sergers have as many as 5 needle positions.

There are specialized 4-thread sergers now available that have the left needle(s) that chain, and/or cover hem, at a separate time from overlocking.

The basic serger stitch is the overlock. The overlock needle positions are very important because they also help determine the width of the overlock stitch. When the outside needle is used, the stitch width forms wider, using all the stitch fingers. When the inside needle is used alone, the stitch is narrower.

Some sergers require special or industrial type needles while others can use the many types of sewing machine needles available. Most sergers will allow for needle sizes in the range of 75/11 to 90/14, but a few will accommodate smaller or larger needles. Consult your owner's manual or local dealer.

It is important to change the needles in your serger often. Failure to do so will not only damage your fabric, but can cause breakage and snagging of decorative threads.

The Parts of Your Serger *(cont.)*

LOOPERS

The loopers in the serger serve as the replacement for the bobbin of the sewing machine. If you have a 3 or 4-thread serger then you have an upper and a lower looper. A 5-thread has an extra looper called the chain looper. All loopers are directly fed with thread.

upper looper
directs the thread in a "zig zag" manner, across the top, or upper side, of the fabric edge. It is also called the top looper.

chain looper
carries the thread in an oval pattern to form the lower, or underside, of the chain stitch and/or cover hem stitch. It is also called the front looper.

lower looper
directs the thread, in a "zig zag" manner, across the underside of the fabric edge. Your owner's manual may also call this the bottom looper.

DIFFERENTIAL FEED

Differential feed is a fabric compensator. It can aid in sewing different types of fabrics, different weights of fabrics and different areas of the fabric/garment resulting in a flat and smooth seam or edge. It can also aid in completing some techniques.

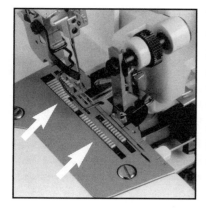 The differential feed is accomplished by the use of a two-part feed dog system – front and back sets. The feed dogs for regular serging run at the same rate (setting 1 or "N"). In the "positive" (higher number/+) or "negative" (lower number/-) feeding, both feed dogs operate at different rates. The "positive" feeding creates a pushing action, while the "negative" feeding results in a pulling action.

For light weight or single layer fabrics, that might pucker when serged at a "normal" setting, adjust the setting for more "negative" feeding (lower number/-) and it acts as if you are holding the fabric taut in front and behind the foot. The serged edge will lay smoother. For stretchy fabrics and/or grainlines, single or more fabric layers, where the serged edge is wavy and stretched out; adjust the differential feed setting to a "positive" feeding (higher number/+) and the serged edge will lay smoother.

The following jingle may help you remember which way to adjust the system for normal smooth sewing/construction:

The LOWER the number, the LIGHTER the fabric.
The HIGHER the number, the HEAVIER the stretch.

NOTE:
Instructions in this book leave this setting up to you because it directly relates to the fabric and the area you are serging. Always test the technique on the project fabric in the exact grainline it will be used.

What Tensions Should Look Like

In this section, basic machine set up for each type of serger configuration (stitch) is outlined to help you understand what each tension type looks like when adjusted correctly. I describe them by look, not by what to adjust, because different types of threads on different machines will require different adjustments.

3-Thread Stitch

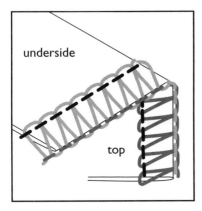

1. The upper looper thread should lay flat and snake across the top of the fabric.

2. The lower looper thread should lay flat on the underside, and look like a sideways "V".

3. The needle thread should look like a straight stitch from the top side and a dot at the bottom of the "V" on the underside. The "V"s are connected by a straight looking stitch at the bottom.

4. The upper looper and lower looper threads should balance in the middle on the edge of the fabric.

SERGER SET-UP:	*3–Thread Stitch*
MACHINE SET-UP:	wide plate/stitch finger
THREAD:	left* overlock needle: regular or cone thread to coordinate with decorative thread and/or fabric
	upper looper: decorative thread
	lower looper: decorative thread (optional, see design note below) or regular, or cone thread
KNIFE/CUTTER:	usually cutting/engaged, unless indicated
LENGTH:	1-2 based on weight of decorative thread and desired effect

*If you have a 5-thread serger you may have two right needle positions and at least one left (front) needle position. The right (back) positions are the overlock needles and for this stitch type you should use the outside (left) of this needle position. There are 4-thread sergers that form a 3-thread stitch using only the right overlock needle. If you have questions, consult your owner's manual and/or dealer.

DESIGN NOTE:
In this type of serger set-up you can choose to put the decorative thread in the upper looper, or for a reversible effect, use decorative thread in both loopers. If only one decorative thread is desired, then use it only in the upper looper with coordinating thread in the lower looper.

NARROW HEM AND ROLLED HEM

Ready-to-wear uses two types of narrow finishes:

1. Narrow edge or hem– uses a narrow stitch finger/plate but normal/regular "look" tensions. Fabric may, or may not, roll. This is done in 3-thread only.

2. Rolled edge or hem– uses a narrow stitch finger/plate/foot but a tight lower looper tension that causes most fabrics to roll. The thread from the front rolls around to the back. This can be completed in 2 or 3-thread.

These two can be interchangeable, but some types of fabric techniques and personal taste will determine whether narrow hem or rolled hem would be better.

Narrow Hem or Edge

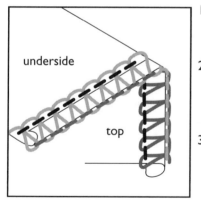

1. The upper looper thread should lay flat on the top side of the fabric.

2. The lower looper thread should lay flat on the underside and look like a sideways "V".

3. The needle thread should look like a straight stitch from the top side and a dot at the bottom of the "V" on the underside.

4. The upper looper and lower looper threads should balance in the middle on the edge of the fabric.

5. The stitches are narrow in width and close together, similar to a satin stitch.

SERGER SET-UP:	*Narrow Hem or Edge*
MACHINE SET-UP:	narrow stitch finger/plate/foot; adjust fixed cutter as manual indicates
THREAD:	right* overlock needle: regular or cone thread to coordinate with decorative thread and/or fabric
	upper looper: decorative thread
	lower looper: regular or cone thread to coordinate with decorative thread
KNIFE/CUTTER:	usually engaged, unless otherwise indicated
LENGTH:	1-2 based on weight of decorative thread and desired effect

*There are a few brands/models of sergers that require the use of the left overlock needle for a narrow hem/edge, not the right. If you have any questions consult your instruction manual or local dealer. If your serger has two right (back) needle positions (usually a 5-thread serger) you are to use the inside (right) needle of this position. If you have questions, please consult your manual or dealer.

ROLLED HEM OR EDGE

This technique can be completed using 2 or 3 threads. Most sergers have 3-thread capabilities, but not all have 2-thread capabilities. A rolled hem done in 2-threads will look similar on the front and back, while a 3-thread rolled hem has a small ridge, or extra thread, that appears on the back, against the fabric.

2-Thread Rolled Hem or Edge Stitch

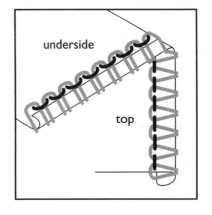

1. The lower looper thread should wrap the fabric edge tightly, rolling from the front to the back. The thread should lay securely against the fabric on the top and the underside.

2. The needle thread forms a short straight stitch line on the top and helps hold the looper thread secure against the underside of the fabric.

3. The stitches are narrow in width and close together, similar to a satin stitch.

3-Thread Rolled Hem or Edge Stitch

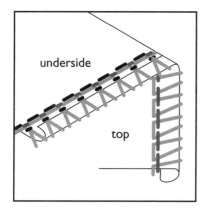

underside

top

1. The upper looper thread is covering the edge by rolling from the front to the back.

2. The needle thread forms a short straight stitch line on the top and holds both looper threads securely against the underside of the fabric.

3. The lower looper thread looks like it has disappeared on the underside of the fabric, in a ridge, against the fabric.

4. The stitches are narrow in width and close together, similar to a satin stitch.

SERGER SET-UP: *Rolled Hem or Edge*

MACHINE SET-UP: narrow stitch finger/plate/foot; fixed cutter adjustment as manual indicates

THREAD: right* overlock needle: regular or cone thread to coordinate with decorative thread and/or fabric

upper looper: decorative thread for 3-thread; 2-thread converter for 2-thread

lower looper: 3-thread, use regular or cone thread to coordinate with decorative thread or fabric; 2-thread, use decorative thread

KNIFE/CUTTER: usually engaged, unless otherwise indicated

LENGTH: 1-2 based on weight of decorative thread and desired effect

*There are a few brands/model of sergers that require the use of the left overlock needle for a narrow hem/edge, not the right. If you have any questions consult your instruction manual or local dealer. If your serger has two right (back) needle positions (usually a 5-thread serger) you are to use the inside (right) needle of this position. If you have questions, please consult your manual or dealer.

Helpful Hint: If you have both 2 and 3-thread options on your serger... choose 2-thread rolled hem/edge if the decorative thread is light to medium weight... choose 3-thread rolled hem if the decorative thread is heavy weight or if you are having problems with the decorative thread stitching consistently.

FLATLOCK

This technique looks like a bad seam that pulls open. It is stitched on a fold, or an edge, then pulled open to complete. It can be completed using 2 or 3 threads. Most sergers have 3-thread capabilities, but not all have 2-thread capabilities. Flatlock completed in 2-threads may lay flatter; while 3-thread flatlock has a small ridge or extra thread that appears on the front against the fabric.

*There are two sides to the flatlock stitch... the **loops** side that looks like a looper stitch and the **ladder** side, like the rungs of a ladder. Both are considered the right side depending on the desired effect.*

When you want the loops side of the flatlock to show, the fabric is placed wrong sides together before being sewn.

2-Thread Flatlock

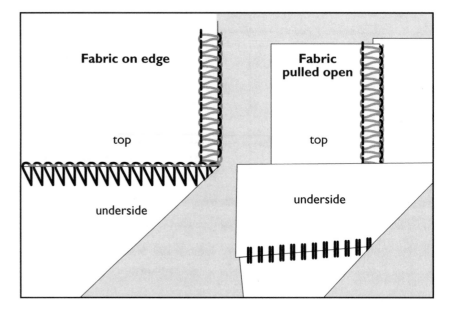

Fabric on edge — top — underside

Fabric pulled open — top — underside

1. The needle thread should look like a straight stitch from the top and a smooth "V" across the underside of the fabric.

2. The lower looper thread should look smooth and snake across the top side of the fabric.

3. The two threads should interlock *exactly* on the edge of the fabric.

3-Thread Flatlock

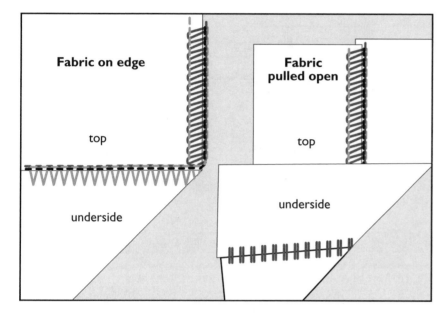

1. The needle thread should look like a straight stitch from the top and make a smooth "V" across the underside of the fabric.

2. The upper looper thread should look smooth and snake across the upper or top side of the fabric.

3. All threads interlock, balanced *exactly* on the edge of the fabric.

4. The lower looper thread should appear to "disappear" or bury itself in the locking threads on the edge. This may create a slight ridge on the loop side.

SERGER SET-UP: *Flatlock*

MACHINE SET-UP: wide stitch finger/plate/foot; 2-thread converter on upper looper (for 2-thread only)

THREAD: left* overlock needle: regular or cone thread to coordinate with decorative thread or fabric

upper looper: decorative thread for 3-thread; 2-thread converter for 2-thread

lower looper: 3-thread, use regular or cone thread to coordinate with decorative thread or fabric; 2-thread, use decorative thread

KNIFE/CUTTER: usually disengaged/non-cutting, unless otherwise indicated

LENGTH: 1.5-2.5 based on weight of decorative thread and desired effect

*If you have a 5-thread serger, you may have two right (back) needle positions and at least one left (front) needle position. The right (back) positions are the overlock needles and for this technique you are to use the outside (left) needle of this position.

There are some 4-thread sergers that only 3-thread using the right overlock needle. If you have questions, please consult your manual or local dealer.

HELPFUL HINT:
For decorative serging on the loops side, with a light to medium-weight novelty thread, use it in the lower looper and choose 2-thread flatlock. If using a heavier decorative thread or if having trouble with the decorative thread, use a 3-thread flatlock.

REVERSE FLATLOCK

Reverse flatlock uses the ladder side of the stitch. The tension look is the same, but the decorative threads are in a different place. This technique can be completed using 2 or 3-thread machine set up.

When using the reverse/ladder side of flatlock, fabric is placed right sides together before being sewn.

SERGER SET-UP:	*Reverse Flatlock*
MACHINE SET-UP:	wide stitch finger/plate/foot; size 16/100 Universal or 12/80 or 14/90 metallic (*Metallica; Metafil; Metalfil*) or Topstitch 90/14 or 100/16 needle**; 2-thread converter on upper looper [for 2-thread flatlock only]
THREAD:	left* overlock needle: decorative thread
	upper looper: (for 3-thread only) serger thread to match fabric color
	lower looper: thread to match fabric color
KNIFE/CUTTER:	usually disengaged/non-cutting, unless otherwise indicated
LENGTH:	1.5-4 based on weight of decorative thread, technique and desired effect

*If you have a 5-thread serger, you may have two right (back) needle positions and at least one left (front) needle position. The right (back) positions are the overlock needles and for this technique you are to use the outside (left) needle of the right (back) position. There are some 4-thread sergers that only 3-thread using the right overlock needle. If you have questions, please consult your manual or local dealer.

**Use these needles only if your serger is designed to use regular sewing machine needles. If special serger needles are required, use size 90/14. Consult your manual or local dealer if you have questions.

Helpful Hint:
If you have both 2 and 3-thread options on your serger…
2-thread flatlock usually lays flatter. Choose 3-thread flatlock
if the stitch does not want to form or if you are having prob-
lems with keeping the decorative thread stitching consistently.

CHAIN STITCH

This is a straight stitch formed by the serger. It uses 2 threads and a different looper system than regular overlocking. It is not available on all sergers. Some older sergers that chain stitch do not have the ability to drop the upper looper and sew anywhere on the fabric. If you have one of these sergers, do not attempt to use decorative chain stitching as various techniques suggest. For decorative uses, serge with the wrong side of the fabric up so the chain loops show.

Chain Stitch

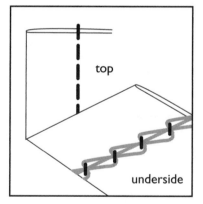

1. The needle thread should look like a conventional straight stitch from the top. From the underside, the needle secures the looper thread tightly to the fabric.

2. The looper thread makes little tight oval stitches on the underside of the fabric. The oval loops should lay smoothly and tightly against the back side of the fabric.

SERGER SET-UP:	*Chain Stitch*
MACHINE SET-UP:	drop upper looper; attach flat sewing surface; etc. - see instructions in your manual for other specifics and the proper order to complete the machine set-up
THREAD:	chain needle: regular or cone thread to coordinate with decorative thread chain looper: decorative thread; for types and weights of decorative threads recommended for decorative chain stitching, see charts on pages 30 and 31.
KNIFE/CUTTER:	disengaged/non-cutting
LENGTH:	2.5-4.0 based on weight of decorative thread and desired effect

COVER HEM

This is a stitch that is relatively new to the home sergers. The term might be new, but what the stitch looks like is not. It is frequently used to hem commercial knit garments but has many other uses. Presently, it is only available on newer and top end sergers.

It has two or three rows of stitching on the top and an overlock, braid-like look from the underside. It is sewn flat, not on a folded edge. For decorative uses, sew with the wrong side of the fabric up.

Cover Hem

Triple Cover Hem

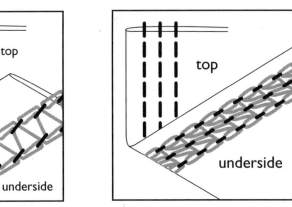

SERGER SET-UP:	*Cover Hem*
MACHINE SET-UP:	drop upper looper; attach flat sewing surface; etc. - see instructions in your manual for other specifics and the proper order to complete the machine set-up
THREAD:	cover hem needles: regular or cone thread to coordinate with decorative thread
	cover hem looper: decorative thread; for types and weights of decorative threads recommended for decorative chain stitching, see charts on pages 30 and 31
KNIFE/CUTTER:	disengaged/non-cutting
LENGTH:	2.5-4.0 based on weight of decorative thread and desired effect

1. The needle threads should look like straight stitches on the top and secure the looper thread tightly to the underside of the fabric.

2. The looper thread forms parallel chain-like stitches, on the underside of the fabric, while snaking smoothly back and forth.

Decorative Thread Library

The simplest way to be creative with your serger is to use decorative threads in the looper(s). These decorative threads, combined with the various DecoSerging techniques, will add panache to your project.

This section is about some of the assorted decorative threads that are available at your local sewing supply store or by mail order. This is not a complete list, but these are the threads that have been tested by the author and found to work successfully on most brands of sergers. Feel free to experiment with other threads!

Reference to the threads on this list, by weight, will be used for the various techniques in the sections to follow.

The name of the thread will be followed by the manufacturer in most cases. Some of the decorative threads are listed together because they are very similar, but are from different manufacturers.

Attachments will be noted for certain threads where needed for more successful results.

LIGHT WEIGHT DECORATIVE THREADS

These threads will fit easily through the eye of the needle and/or any looper.

MACHINE EMBROIDERY THREADS:
Rayon threads: *Finishing Touch* by Finishing Touch; Madeira brand; *Mega Sheen; Radianté* by Hoop It All; *Scansilk* by Sullivans; *Signature* by American and Efird; *Sulky* by Sulky of America; *Color Twist* by Coats & Clark; Coats & Clark brand; Gütermann brand

Acrylic: Janome brand; *Ultrasheen* by YLI Corp.; Brother brand

Cotton: DMC brand; Mettler/Metrosene brand; *Cotona* by Madeira

Polyester: *Neon* by Madeira; *Perfect Image* by Finishing Touch

Metallic: Madeira brand; Sulky brand; YLI brand; *Scanfil* by Sullivans; Coats & Clark brand; *Signature* by American and Efird; Gütermann brand

Embroidery thread is different from regular thread because it is designed to be decorative rather than strong. Sewing threads have a high twist for strength but do not lay as smooth and silky.

Decorative Thread Library *(cont.)*

Embroidery threads have a low twist so they will have a more satin-like sheen when stitched. Embroidery threads are made in rayon, acrylic, polyester or cotton, and are available in various weights. The thread weight is usually labeled on the spool or thread rack. Some brands are made in more than one weight, so make a note of which you are using. The larger the number, the finer the thread. For example: 30 weight thread is thicker and has more coverage than a 40 weight thread.

The fiber content of the thread will determine the strength of the thread. Since polyester is the strongest fiber used for machine embroidery threads, the embroidery threads that will serge with the least breakage are the brands made from polyester.

Perfect Image is a lubricated polyester thread, where the lubricant washes out and the thread "puffs" up after laundering. This creates more thread coverage.

Color Twist from Coats & Clark is a 35 weight rayon thread that has two colored rayon threads twisted together to make one thread. When stitched out, the colors blend together to create a unique effect.

Metallic threads do not have a weight listed on the spool like fiber embroidery threads. These threads are made of a coated plastic sheet, or thin metallic strip, wrapped around a natural or synthetic core. When serging with metallics in the needle, it is highly recommended to always use a new needle so the thread does not shred or split. If your serger can use sewing machine needles, use a *Metafil, Metalfil, Metallic,* or *Metallica* needle with these threads to help prevent breakage.

Madeira has a metallic called *Super Twist.* It is a textured, twisted metallic thread. It looks great alone or blended with other threads for a hint of shine.

It is especially helpful to use either a *Decorative Thread Holder* or the *ThreadPRO* (see Helpful Accessories) when serging with metallics. This will allow the thread to feed off the spool properly and prevent twisting and breakage.

Sliver by Sulky
Tinsel Thread by Stream Lame
Glitz by Coats and Clark

These threads are a wider, flat metallic thread that looks like narrow Christmas tree tinsel; available in lots of colors. These products serge with more texture and higher luster than regular metallic thread.

Jewel by Madeira
Prism by Glissen Gloss

These are variations on the *Sliver, Tinsel Thread* and *Glitz* threads and have a holographic surface that reflects the light in a unique way.

Both type of tinsel threads, with and without hologram, feed off better horizontally or flat. This will prevent the twisting, stretching and breaking that occurs easily with these threads. Either use the *ThreadPRO* or a *Decorative Thread Holder* as an accessory to feed the thread horizontally.

INVISIBLE THREADS

Invisible Nylon Thread by Sew Art Int.
Premium Invisible Thread by Sulky
Wonder Invisible Thread by YLI
Monofil by Madeira
Transparent by Signature

These products are a very thin transparent thread used for their ability to hide so the other decorative thread will show. *Invisible Nylon Thread* and *Wonder Invisible Threads* are nylon while *Premium Invisible Thread* and *Monofil* are polyester. They are all available in clear and smoke colors. Use the smoke color when serging with dark decorative threads so this thread will disappear and not shine or reflect light.

MEDIUM WEIGHT DECORATIVE THREADS

These threads will work well through most loopers, but do not always fit through the needle eye.

Decor 6 by Madeira
Designer 6 by YLI

These threads work well in large eye needles and all loopers (upper, lower, chain and cover hem). They are like an untwisted, rayon pearl cotton. These threads have a beautiful look but due to the low twist and fiber content, are not very durable. Elect to use them in places on your project that get little friction because of the very low abrasion resistance of the loose, untwisted fibers.

Candlelight by YLI
Glamour by Madeira

These threads easily work in the upper, lower, and chain loopers, and on some cover hem loopers. They are light weight metallic yarn-like products. *Glamour* is slightly lighter weight or softer than *Candlelight*. Most of the *Candlelight* colors are solids, while *Glamour* has mostly multi-colors.

As with metallic threads, metallic yarns feed off the spool smoother when allowed to feed horizontal flat. Use either a *Decorative Thread Holder* or the *ThreadPRO* to accomplish this.

Renaissance by Sew Art Int.
Success, Monét by YLI

These threads work well in large eye needles and all loopers (upper, lower, chain, and cover hem). They are very thin, "hairy" yarn-like threads. *Success* is 100% acrylic and a little thicker, while *Renaissance* and *Monét* are wool and acrylic blends.

Jeans Stitch by YLI

This thread works well in a large eye needle and all loopers (upper, lower, chain and cover hem). It is a highly twisted, size 30, thicker polyester thread that resembles topstitching thread in thickness. It is available in solids and one variegated color. Due to the high twist and fiber content, *Jeans Stitch* is very durable.

Pearl Crown Rayon by YLI

This thread is a highly twisted rayon cord-like thread, like a pearl cotton, but with more luster. Pearl Crown Rayon is fairly durable in wear, but it should be hung to dry, due to the rayon fiber content. It works very well on these loopers: upper, lower and chain. It can be used on some sergers in the cover hem looper, too. It is available in solids and five variegated colors.

Metroflock by Mettler
Rainbow Thread by New Home
Woolly Nylon by YLI
Woolly Nylon Extra by YLI

These products work well on all loopers (upper, lower, chain and cover hem). They are texturized, nylon yarns. *Metroflock, Woolly Nylon* and *Woolly Nylon Extra* are available in many solid colors. *Woolly Nylon* and *Rainbow Thread* have additional multi-colors, while only *Wooly Nylon* has a metallic version. These products are used not only for decorative work, but they will increase the coverage of an edge more than a regular thread. Because these threads naturally add tension, they can also be used to add tension in a looper for better results on a technique, or to improve tension adjustment with other decorative threads. *Woolly Nylon Extra* is three times as bulky as the regular weight and can be used for more coverage and more tension.

HEAVY WEIGHT DECORATIVE THREADS

These are the heaviest threads that will run easily through your serger. They are to be used in the upper and lower looper only.

Ribbon Thread by MDG

Ribbon Thread is a cross-woven knitting ribbon made of 100% rayon solid colors and metallics. It is available in 72 colors including a variety of metallics and three wider multi-color metallics. These multi-color metallics are a little wide and too stiff to easily work in the serger, but are great to weave with for reverse flatlock and wide cover hem. *Ribbon Thread* is available in 10 meter (usually not enough to serge any distance, but enough yardage to weave with) and 100 meter spools.

Ribbon Floss

This thread is also a cross woven knitting ribbon. It is available in 40 yard spools of rayon solids and 30 yard spools of metallics.

NOVELTY THREADS

These threads are just what the title suggests. Most are not usually used for serging, but are great for adding texture and interest to various techniques. Described below are a few you may find at your local sewing store or favorite mail-order source.

Designer Threads by Threadline
Designer Threads is a card of novelty yarn or cord like threads. Each card is color coordinated and has a mixture of textures. The cards have 5 different threads, 10 yards each.

On The Surface by On The Surface
These cards are wrapped with coordinating novelty cords and yarns. Each card has 6 types of threads, in 5 yard lengths. On the back of the cards are instructions for different "fiber manipulation" lessons.

Plumetes, Chenille, Bouclé, Eyelash, Marabout by Quilter's Resource Inc.
These are individual 10 yard length packages of specialty yarns. They come in a variety of colors, types, textures and fiber contents. They all will add color to the cover hem and reverse flatlock.

Silk Ribbon by YLI
This is a soft, woven, narrow silk ribbon that is most often used for hand embroidery. However, it is great for weaving in reverse flatlock. It is available in lots of colors and in widths from 2-7mm and various yardage lengths.

Thread Fuse by YLI; *Stitch and Fuse* by Coats & Clark
These are melt-adhesive threads. When steam is applied, the "glue" thread melts and adheres to the project, leaving a polyester thread behind to hold the stitch together.

Carat by Madeira
This is a knitted metallic braid-like ribbon. It is very flexible for weaving and knotting in reverse flatlock or cover hem.

Spark Organdy by YLI
This is a 100% nylon ribbon in 5mm and 9mm widths. As the name indicates, it is made of a sheer sparkle organdy which creates very interesting effects when woven in reverse flatlock, cross-woven reverse flatlock and cover hem.

Decorative Thread Library *(cont.)*

WHAT THREAD FOR WHAT STITCH?

STITCH TYPES

THREAD	3-T Overlock	Flatlock	Reverse Flatlock**	Narrow/Rolled Hem	Chain Stitch	Cover Hem
machine embroidery-rayon, cotton, acrylic, polyester	X	X	X	X	X	X
machine embroidery-metallics	X	X	X	X	X*	X*
monofilament/invisible	X	X	X	X	X	X*
Sliver, Tinsel Thread, Glitz	X	X	X	X	X*	X*
Prism, Jewel	X	X	X	X	X*	X*
Decor 6; Designer 6	X	X	X	X	X	X
Candlelight, Glamour	X	X	NO	X	X	X***
Success, Renaissance, Monét	X	X	X	X	X	X
Jeans Stitch	X	X	X	X	X	X
Pearl Crown Rayon	X	X	X****	X	X	X***
Woolly Nylon, Metroflock, Rainbow	X	X	X	X	X	X
Woolly Nylon Extra	X	X	X	X	X	X
Ribbon Thread, Ribbon Floss	X	X	NO	NO	NO	NO

* may break easily
** recommend to use a metallic needle (*Metallica, Metafil, Metallic* or *Metalfil*), or Topstitch needle
***can be used, but not in all brands or models of sergers
****possible on some sergers with the use of a size 100 Topstitch or 90 *Metafil* needle
Consult owner's manual or dealer if you can use this size needle in your serger.

WHAT THREADS GO WHERE?

THREAD	TYPE	LOOPER USE	NEEDLE
machine embroidery-rayon, cotton, acrylic, polyester	light weight	CL;CH;UL;LL	yes
machine embroidery-metallics	light weight	UL;LL;CL*;CH*	yes*
monofilaments	lightweight	CL;UL;LL	yes
Sliver, Tinsel Thread, Glitz	light weight	CL;CH;UL;LL	yes*
Prism, Jewel	lightweight	CL;CH;UL;LL	yes*
Decor 6; Designer 6	light weight	CL;CH;UL;LL	yes**
Candlelight, Glamour	medium	CL;UL;LL;CH**	no
Success, Renaissance	medium	CL;CH;UL;LL	yes**
Jeans Stitch	medium	CL;CH;UL;LL	yes**
Pearl Crown Rayon	medium	CL;UL;LL;CH***	yes****
Woolly Nylon, Metroflock, Rainbow	medium	CL;CH;UL;LL	yes
Woolly Nylon Extra	medium	CL;CH;UL;LL	no
Ribbon Thread, Ribbon Floss	heavy	UL;LL	no

KEY:

CL-chain looper

CH-cover hem looper

UL-upper looper

LL-lower looper

* may break easily
** recommend to use a metallic needle (*Metallica, Metafil, Metallic* or *Metalfil*) or Topstitch needle
***can be used, but not in all brands or models of sergers
****possible on some sergers with the use of a size 100 Topstitch or 90 *Metafil* needle

Helpful Accessories

This section contains notions and accessories that are useful for either your general serging and/or your decorative serging. Like most notions they make a job easier or help you complete a project with better results.

blind hem foot

This foot, for most brands, has an adjustable guide on it that directs a fabric edge right into the needle. This is a popular accessory because it can be the best seam guide for detail and precise serging. It is suggested for many techniques.

seam guide

As the name suggests, this accessory is designed to guide an edge of fabric into the cutting/sewing area. Some serger models come with a seam guide while others have this available as an extra accessory. The design of the guide available for your serger may allow you to adjust where the fabric edge is guided, while others are preset by the manufacturer. Adjustable guides are more versatile, but like most serger accessories, they are not interchangeable from one brand to another.

Threader Set

This specific brand is a set of handy threaders for all kinds of loopers, for threading both regular and decorative threads. The long-handled, thin, twisted wire type is especially useful.

floss threader

This is a drug store item used to thread floss between teeth, but it is also very helpful when threading difficult decorative threads through the looper eyes.

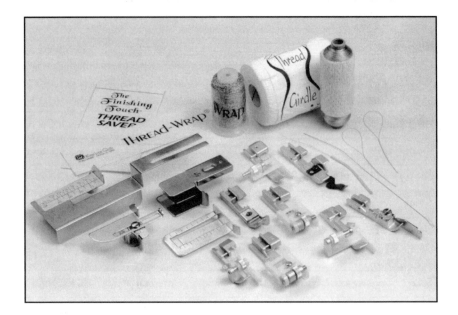

Thread Wrap by Katie Lane Quilts
Thread Saver by Finishing Touch

These vinyl strips wrap around the thread spool after they have been partially used and prevent the remaining thread from coming off the spool.

Thread Girdle by *ThreadPRO*

Use this elastic material to wrap around a thread spool after it has been partially used. This product keeps the leftover thread from coming off the spool. It can also be used on threads during serging to keep the thread from unwinding off the spool and getting caught on the spool pin.

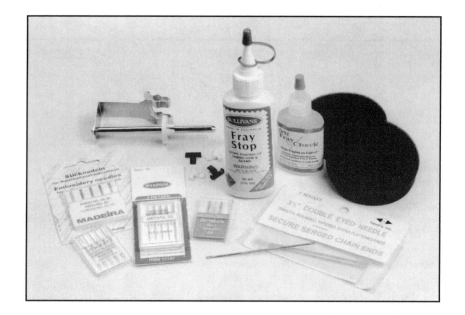

Tail Tucker (double-eyed needle)

This notion has many applications, but is called a *Tail Tucker* because its primary use is to tuck the serger chain "tail" back through the sewn seam. This prevents the end of the seam from coming apart and unraveling. It can also be used to weave ribbons through faggoting and reverse flatlock. The *Tail Tucker* is flat at both ends so it weaves and slides through threads more easily than a large eye tapestry needle.

seam sealant

This is a liquid that, when applied, and allowed to dry, will prevent the cut serged seam from unraveling. It is semi-permanent. *(Fray Check; No Fray; Fray Stop)*

Decorative Thread Holder

This is an extra spool holder that fits on the thread antenna. It helps the thread feed more smoothly off the spool horizontally. The fact that the holder is horizontal, reduces the chance of the thread getting wrapped around the spool pin as it slips off the spool. This accessory is very helpful with all metallic products.

foam pads or cushions

These fit on the thread spool pins to help stabilize cone thread. When using a regular machine spool type, or decorative threads, they help prevent the thread from getting under the spool and getting caught on the spool pin. It is recommended that you have one for each spool position.

specialty needles

These are needles other than the normal serger needles. They are used to help with a specialized thread or to aid in a technique. Please note that all the specialized needles mentioned are designed for the sewing machine, and some sergers require the use of only a special serger needle. Consult your owner's manual or local dealer if you have questions. Use a metallic needle *(Metafil, Metalfil, Metallica or Metallic)* with metallic thread. With embroidery thread, use an Embroidery needle. A Quilting needle will help when quilt piecing on the serger. A metallic or Topstitch needle may help when using a larger thread through the eye for reverse flatlock.

Helpful Accessories *(cont.)*

Tension Release Clip

This is a plastic clip that is inserted at the first thread guide from the antenna. It slips under the guide to relieve some tension on the thread, thus eliminating some of the tension adjustment required when working with decorative threads. This accessory was designed by ELNA and is included with some of their models. It can be used very successfully with various other models and brands.

ThreadPRO

This is a thread delivery system stand that is designed to take thread off the spool the same way the manufacturer put it on, horizontally and flat. This delivery system solves the problem of breaking, stretching, and twisting for all kinds of threads. It can solve problems for the serger in the same way it solves them for sewing machines. Most metallic threads and yarn-like products are especially helped by the use of this product. The horizontal bar on the stand is long enough for you to put two regular size spools on at the same time and blend your own colors, too.

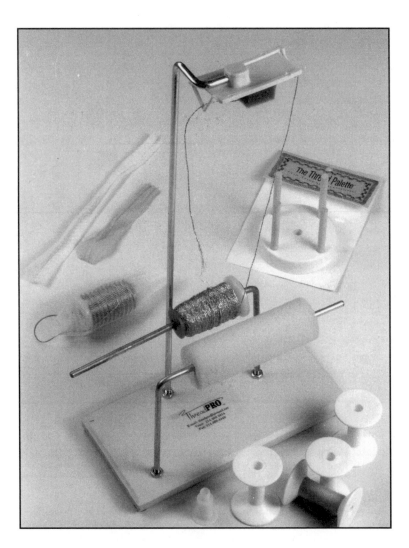

Commercial Cone Adapter

This is an accessory for the *ThreadPRO* stand. It is used for larger cones of metallic and invisible threads so the cone will feed the thread off smoothly and correctly (horizontally). The foam portion of this attachment can also be removed to expose another horizontal bar. Use this in conjunction with the original horizontal bar, to blend as many as four threads through the same looper.

Thread Palette

This novelty accessory slips onto the spool pin and has four small spool pins of its own that allow you to blend different threads together in the same looper. You can be creative and mix your own palette of colors, just like a painter.

E-Z Winder

This product comes with a winding adapter and four empty spools which allows you to use other specialized yarns and cords on your serger. Use the adapter on the bobbin winder of your sewing machine to spin the spool while filling them with all sorts of threads. You can also use it to save money on your regular cone thread by winding off the thread from one cone to several for all thread positions.

spool netting

This is a plastic mesh net that is used around thread spools to prevent too much thread from slipping off the spool during serging. When using this product, make sure it does not get caught on the thread, slip off the spool and get caught at the antenna.

Helpful Hints for DecoSerging

You now have all the tools for the techniques, but before you start, here are some helpful hints for successful decorative serging.

■ When using decorative threads, serge slower than normal for more control. If your serger has a speed control on the machine or the foot control, set it at slow.

■ When chaining off without fabric, hold the thread tail taut, both before the project reaches the needle and after. This will prevent the heavier decorative threads from building up on the stitch finger. This is known as "stacking". If too much thread has built up, it will push the build up on the project or jam the fabric on the machine.

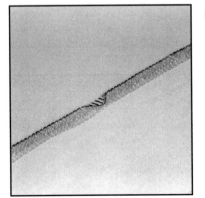

■ "Hiccups", or skipped stitches, are caused from uneven feeding of the thread. Try changing the spool from horizontal to vertical or vice versa. See the box "Problems with Consistent Tensions", at the end of this section for other things to look for.

■ Follow these steps in setting up your serger with a decorative thread spool or a traditional sewing spool. First, take off the cone holder. Next, put a cushion or foam pad on the spool pin, then replace the thread on the pin and use a spool cap on the top of the spool to prevent the thread from tangling or not feeding smoothly. For a spool cap to fit properly and work effectively, it

should not sit at the top like a "hat", but it must slide down to the spool. If your brand provides the "hat" style, I suggest you replace them with ones that are more effective.

■ When adjusting tensions for all techniques, you do not have to test sew with the use of large scraps of your fabric, as this will only waste your decorative thread. However, after making all tension adjustments, always make a final test on a long strip of your project fabric before going on to the real project. This long test should show any irregularities that didn't appear in short tests.

■ Try to skim the raw edge of the fabric with the cutter to trim off the "fuzzies" for a smooth, even-edge finish. (*Omit this hint if the technique requires the cutter disengaged.*)

■ While setting tensions for a technique with decorative thread, leave the cutter engaged and let the cutter skim off the edge of your testing fabric. This edge will give you a true read on whether the tensions look correct. After the tensions are correctly set, disengage the cutter if needed for the technique (ex: flatlock).

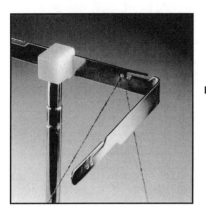

■ If your serger antenna has a separate small hole, thread this when using decorative threads. This will keep it from getting tangled with other threads.

■ When using threads with glued labels on the spool, remove the labels before putting the spool on the spool pin. This will keep the spool pin clean and will let the spool spin freely.

■ No two spools of decorative thread will run through your serger exactly the same way, even if they are the same brand and type.

■ In general, for most stitch types, it takes approximately 7-9 yards of thread to test and adjust your tensions.

■ If you cannot adjust your tensions tight enough to get the correct stitch appearance for a 3-thread rolled hem or flatlock, you can thread the lower looper with *Woolly Nylon*. Due to the nature of this thread, it will add tension.

PROBLEMS WITH INCONSISTENT TENSIONS?
(better known as hiccup cures)

Inconsistent tensions could be due to:

■ too loose tension on the decorative threads.

■ uneven feeding of the thread because it is caught somewhere. Check the thread route; check to see if the thread is feeding off the spool smoothly; may need to use a horizontal thread system such as a *Decorative Thread Holder* or *ThreadPRO* for the thread to feed smoothly.

■ machine not threaded correctly; type of thread.

■ thread not smooth and even*.

■ tension system on serger not feeding consistently*.

■ threads may not be in tension disc.

■ metallic threads or yarn-like products are more wiry so this can cause some irregularities that you may not always be able to completely eliminate*.

* Author's Note:
Sometimes it is nice to know the problems
are not your fault!

Personal DecoSerging Tension Charts

As mentioned at the beginning of the "What Tensions Should Look Like" section, different machines, with different threads, will require different tension settings. It would be impossible to list all brands and models with settings for all different threads, especially with the variation from one spool of thread to another. Therefore, this is to enable you to create your own personal tension/thread reference charts. Take these pages and make copies of the charts. Each time you do a DecoSerging technique, make a note of the settings for the different threads on the correct chart. Next time you use the same type of thread, for the same serger stitch, you will have a tension reference for a starting point. This should save you a lot of set-up time. I suggest you be very specific when filling out the thread information. You will find that as you use more and more types of decorative threads, the charts will also be a helpful guide when trying a new thread.

PERSONAL SERGER SET-UP:
3-Thread Wide

left* overlock needle tension _____

thread type _____

upper looper tension _____

deco thread type _____

lower looper tension _____

deco thread type** _____

fabric _____

---

*If you have a 5-thread serger you **may** have two right (back) needle positions. These are the overlock needles and for this technique you are to use the outside (left) needle of this position. If you have any questions, consult your owner's manual and/or dealer. If you have a 4-thread serger where the left needle looks like a separate stitch from the front, then use the right needle.

**In this type of serger set-up you can choose to put the decorative thread in the upper looper; or for a reversible effect, use decorative thread in both loopers.

PERSONAL SERGER SET-UP:
3-Thread

right* overlock needle tension _____

thread type _____

upper looper tension _____

deco thread type _____

lower looper tension _____

deco thread type** _____

fabric _____

PERSONAL SERGER SET-UP:
3-Thread Rolled Hem

right* overlock needle tension _____

thread type _____

upper looper tension _____

deco thread type _____

lower looper tension _____

thread type _____

fabric _____

*If you have a 5-thread serger you **may** have two right (back) needle positions. These are the overlock needles and for this technique you are to use the inside (right) needle of this position. If you have any questions, consult your owner's manual and/or dealer.
**In this type of serger set-up you can choose to put the decorative thread in the upper looper; or for a reversible effect, use decorative thread in both loopers.

*There are a few brands/models of 4-thread sergers that require the use of the left overlock needle for a rolled hem, not the right. If you have any questions, consult your instruction manual or local dealer.

Personal DecoSerging Tension Charts *(cont.)*

PERSONAL SERGER SET-UP:
2-Thread Rolled Hem

right* overlock needle tension _____

thread type _____

lower looper tension _____

deco thread type _____

fabric _____

*There are a few brands/models of sergers that require the use of the left overlock needle for a rolled hem, not the right. If you have any questions, consult your instruction manual or local dealer.

PERSONAL SERGER SET-UP:
Narrow Hem

right* overlock needle tension _____

thread type _____

upper looper tension _____

deco thread type _____

lower looper tension _____

deco thread type** _____

fabric _____

*There are a few brands/models of sergers that require the use of the left overlock needle for a narrow hem, not the right. If you have any questions, consult your instruction manual or local dealer.

**In this type of serger set-up you can choose to put the decorative thread in the upper looper; or for a reversible effect, use decorative thread in both loopers.

PERSONAL SERGER SET-UP:
3-Thread Flatlock

left* overlock needle tension _____

thread type _____

upper looper tension _____

deco thread type _____

lower looper tension _____

thread type _____

fabric _____

*If you have a 5-thread serger you **may** have two right (back) needle positions. These are the overlock needles and for this technique you are to use the outside (left) needle of this position. If you have any questions, consult your owner's manual and/or dealer.

PERSONAL SERGER SET-UP:
2-Thread Flatlock

left* overlock needle tension _____

thread type _____

lower looper tension _____

deco thread type _____

fabric _____

*If you have a 5-thread serger you **may** have two right (back) needle positions. These are the overlock needles and for this technique you are to use the outside (left) needle of this position. If you have any questions, consult your owner's manual and/or dealer.

Personal DecoSerging Tension Charts *(cont.)*

PERSONAL SERGER SET-UP:
3-Thread Reverse Flatlock

left* overlock needle tension _____

deco thread type _____

upper looper tension _____

thread type _____

lower looper tension _____

thread type _____

fabric _____

*If you have a 5-thread serger you **may** have two right (back) needle positions. These are the overlock needles and for this technique you are to use the outside (left) needle of this position. If you have any questions, consult your owner's manual and/or dealer.

PERSONAL SERGER SET-UP:
2-Thread Reverse Flatlock

left* overlock needle tension _____

deco thread type _____

lower looper tension _____

thread type _____

fabric _____

*If you have a 5-thread serger you **may** have two right (back) needle positions. These are the overlock needles and for this technique you are to use the outside (left) needle of this position. If you have any questions, consult your owner's manual and/or dealer.

PERSONAL SERGER SET-UP:
2-Thread Chain Stitch

chain needle tension _____

thread type _____

chain looper tension _____

deco thread type _____

fabric _____

PERSONAL SERGER SET-UP:
Cover Hem

right cover hem needle tension _____

left cover hem needle tension _____

needle thread _____

cover hem looper tension _____

deco thread type _____

fabric _____

PERSONAL SERGER SET-UP:
Triple Cover Hem

left cover hem needle tension _____

center cover hem needle tension _____

right cover hem needle tension _____

needle thread type _____

cover hem looper tension _____

deco thread type _____

fabric _____

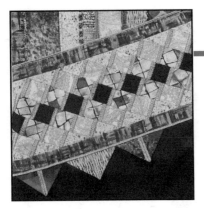

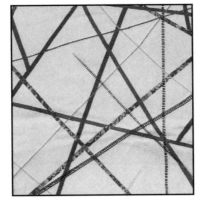

Fabric Techniques

These techniques use fabric or ribbon as the base material. Some of the techniques (such as Serger Lattice, Wavy Lattice and Pick-Up Sticks) create, or recreate, fabric that can be used in your project. Other techniques create texture to be added into a seam (Serger Points or Serger Tabs) or on the surface (Kite Tails) of your project.

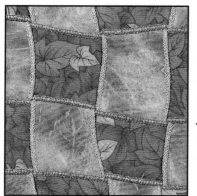

These fabric techniques can be used alone or mixed to create a really one-of-a-kind project.

As with most texturizing techniques, you will complete the decorative work and then cut out the pattern pieces(s) for your project. Exact yardages for supplies are often not given since you will determine the size of the fabric piece you want to create.

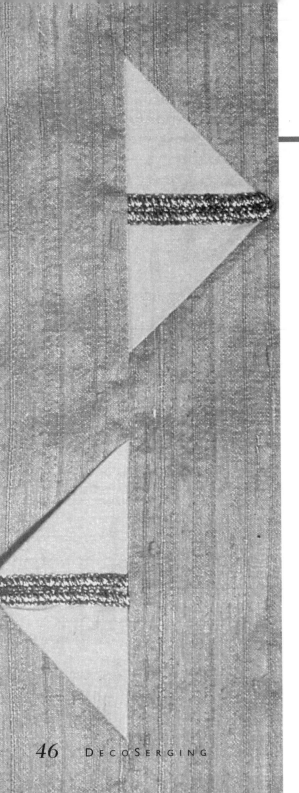

Serger Points – Single Color

These are prairie points–serger style. They can be used in a group or alone and can be tucked into any seam – into a seam while piecing strips, along an edge while putting on a border or to add a novelty edge to a project. There are two types of points: single color and double color.

SUPPLIES

- fabric
- 1 spool of decorative thread
- 1-2 spools/cones of thread (to coordinate with each fabric or decorative thread)
- rotary cutter, ruler, mat

FABRIC PREPARATION

1. Preshrink and press all fabrics.
2. Cut fabrics into 2" strips using a rotary cutter.

(The width of the strip determines how tall the point will be. You can vary the width as needed for your design.)

Design note:
The choice of narrow hem or rolled hem is yours, but narrow hem will lay smoother/flatter than rolled hem.

SERGER SET-UP:	*Rolled or Narrow Hem*
MACHINE SET-UP:	right* overlock needle; a rolled hem plate/stitch finger/foot; 2-thread converter (for 2-thread rolled hem only); fixed cutter adjustment as machine manual instructs
THREAD:	right* overlock needle: matching or coordinating thread
	upper looper: light or medium weight decorative thread if using 3-thread narrow hem/rolled hem; no thread if using 2-thread rolled hem
	lower looper: coordinating thread if using 3-thread narrow hem/rolled hem; decorative thread if using 2-thread rolled hem
KNIFE/CUTTER:	engaged/cutting
DIFFERENTIAL FEED:	1 or "N"
ATTACHMENTS:	none
TENSIONS:	rolled or narrow hem
LENGTH:	1-2, depending on threads and desired effect.

*There are a few serger models that require the use of the left overlock needle for a rolled hem, not the right. If you have any questions consult your instruction manual (see: rolled hem) or your local dealer.

1. With the right side up, serge along one long edge of the fabric strip. Skim the raw edge with the cutter to clean up the "fuzzies".

2A. Fold the strip as follows, starting with the fabric strip wrong side up: Fold the right end down to the unserged, long raw edge. The serged edge should be at a right angle, or perpendicular, to the long edge. Pin in place.

2B. Grasp the serged edge of the strip, to the left of the previously folded edge, and fold down toward you. The serged edges should lay smoothly next to each other. The point is now formed. Pin in place.

3. Cut off the excess strip along the base of the serger point. Baste edges in place and remove pins. Press the point smooth from the wrong side.

Serger Points – Double Color

SUPPLIES

- 2 coordinating fabrics
- 2 spools of decorative thread
- 1 spool/cone of thread
  (to coordinate with
  decorative thread or fabric)
- rotary cutter, ruler, mat

FABRIC PREPARATION

1. Preshrink and press all fabrics.
2. Cut fabrics into 2" strips using
   a rotary cutter.

(The width of the strip determines
how tall the point will be. You can
vary the width as needed for your
design.)

SERGER SET-UP:	*Narrow or Rolled Edge*
MACHINE SET-UP:	right* overlock needle; a rolled hem plate/stitch finger/foot; 2-thread converter (for 2-thread rolled hem only); fixed cutter adjustment as machine manual instructs
THREAD:	right* overlock needle: matching or coordinating thread
	upper looper: light or medium weight decorative thread if using 3-thread narrow hem/rolled hem; no thread if using 2-thread rolled hem
	lower looper: coordinating thread if using 3-thread narrow hem/rolled hem; decorative thread if using 2-thread rolled hem
KNIFE/CUTTER:	engaged/cutting
DIFFERENTIAL FEED:	1 or "N"
ATTACHMENTS:	none
TENSIONS:	rolled or narrow edge
LENGTH:	1-2, depending on thread and desired effect.

*There are a few serger models that require the use of the left overlock needle for a rolled hem, not the right. If you have any questions consult your instruction manual (see: rolled hem) or your local dealer.

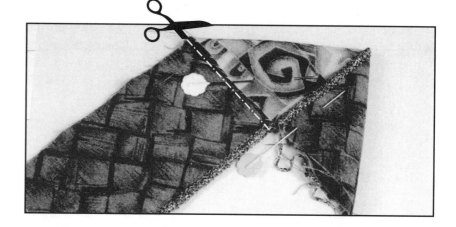

1. Stack two different fabric strips, **wrong** sides together, with edges even.

2. Serge along one long edge of the fabric strips. Skim the raw edge with the cutter, to clean up the "fuzzies".

3A. Fold the double strip as follows: Fold the right end down to the unserged, long raw edge. The serged edge should be at a right angle, or perpendicular, to the raw edge. Pin in place.

3B. Grasp the serged edge of the strip to the left of the previously folded edge and fold under. The serged edge ridges should feel like they lay smoothly next to each other. You should see one fabric on the left side of the point and another fabric on the right side of the point. The point is now formed. Pin in place.

4. Cut off the excess strip along the base of the serger point. Baste edges in place and remove pins. Press the point smooth. Use a press cloth so you will not damage the decorative edge.

ATTACHING TO PROJECT

1. Place the raw edge of the serger point even with the cut edge of the seam allowance, enclosing it into a seam.

2. Sew the seam with a serger or sewing machine.

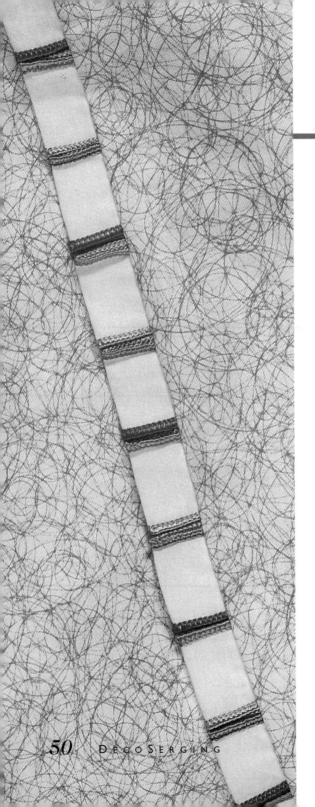

Serger Tabs – Single Color

Serger Tabs, like Serger Points, are made to insert into a seam as added interest or a novelty edge finish. The instructions are for tabs of a single fabric or double fabrics.

SUPPLIES

- tab fabric
- 1 spool of light or medium weight decorative thread
- 1-2 spools of thread to coordinate
- glasshead pins
- rotary cutter, mat and ruler

FABRIC PREPARATION

1. Preshrink and press all fabrics.
2. Cut fabrics into 1½" strips*, using the rotary cutting equipment.

*The width of the strip determines how wide the tab is and this can be varied as needed for your project.

SERGER SET-UP:	*Rolled or Narrow Hem/Edge*
MACHINE SET-UP:	right* overlock needle; rolled hem plate/stitch finger/foot; possible fixed cutter adjustment, as machine manual instructs
THREAD:	right* overlock needle: coordinated thread
	upper looper: light or medium weight decorative thread if using 3-thread narrow hem/rolled hem; no thread if using 2-thread rolled hem
	lower looper: thread to coordinate if using 3-thread narrow hem/rolled hem; decorative thread if using 2-thread rolled hem
KNIFE/CUTTER:	engaged/cutting
DIFFERENTIAL FEED:	1 or "N"
ATTACHMENTS:	none
TENSIONS:	narrow or rolled hem/edge
LENGTH:	1 to 2; depending on thread and desired effect

*There are a few brands/models of sergers that require the use of the left overlock needle for a rolled hem, not the right. If you have any questions consult your instruction manual (see: rolled hem) or your local dealer.

> **Design note:**
> **You can use a rolled hem or narrow edge for this technique, but the narrow hem will lay smoother and be less bulky when the tabs are folded.**

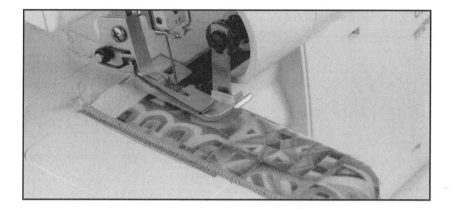 

1. Serge both long edges of the fabric strips. Have the right side of the fabric up as you serge. Skim the edges while serging to cut off the "fuzzies".

2. Measure and cut the serged strip into 3" lengths. This length can vary as desired. The finished tab will be half the length cut minus the seam allowances.

3. Fold the strip in half, wrong sides together, with the two raw ends even. The serged sides should lay on top of each other. Pin raw edges together.

ATTACHING TO PROJECT

1. Place the raw edge of the serger tab even with the cut edge of the seam allowance. Pin or machine baste in place. Place the other project fabric, right sides together, on top.

2. Sew the seam with a serger or sewing machine.

Serger Tabs – Double Color

SUPPLIES

- 2 fabrics
- 2 spools of light or medium weight decorative thread
- 1 spool of thread to coordinate
- glasshead pins
- rotary cutter, mat, and ruler

FABRIC PREPARATION

1. Preshrink and press all fabrics.
2. Cut fabrics into 1½" strips*, using a rotary cutter, mat, ruler

*The width of the strip determines how wide the tab is, and this can be varied as needed for your project.

SERGER SET-UP:	*Narrow Hem/Edge*
MACHINE SET-UP:	right* overlock needle; rolled hem plate/stitch finger, fixed cutter adjustment as machine instructs;
THREAD:	right* overlock needle: matching or coordinating thread
	upper looper: light or medium weight decorative thread
	lower looper: light or medium weight decorative thread
KNIFE/CUTTER:	engaged/cutting
DIFFERENTIAL FEED:	1 or "N", normal
ATTACHMENTS:	none
TENSIONS:	narrow hem
LENGTH:	1 to 2; depending on the threads and desired effect

*There are a few brands/models of sergers that require the use of the left overlock needle for a narrow hem, not the right. If you have any questions consult your instruction manual (see: rolled hem) or your local dealer.

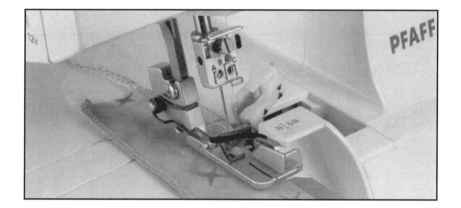 

1. Stack the two strips, one of each fabric, **wrong** sides together with edges even.

2. Serge both long edges of the fabric strips. Have the right side of the main fabric facing up, as you serge. Skim the edges while serging to cut off the "fuzzies".

3. Measure and cut the serged strip into 3" lengths. This length can vary as desired. The finished tab will be approximately half the cut length minus the seam allowances.

4. Fold the strip in half, with the desired fabric on the outside, matching the two raw ends. Then slide the top layer of the tab over to expose the other fabric and serged edge. The amount you slide the fabric over determines how much of the other fabric will be seen.

ATTACHING TO PROJECT

1. Trim edges of the tab straight, if needed.

2. Place the raw edge of the serger tab even with the cut edge of the seam allowance, enclosing it into a seam.

3. Sew the seam with a serger or sewing machine.

Novelty Reverse Flatlock

This technique uses the "ladder" side of flatlock to create the decorative stitch. It really is the most versatile of the flatlock stitches because you can change the look greatly by the thread used in the needle, the stitch length, and by how and what you weave in and out of the "rungs".

SERGER SET-UP:	*2 or 3-Thread Reverse Flatlock*
MACHINE SET-UP:	left* overlock needle; a wide plate/stitch finger/foot; 80/12 or 90/14 metallic needle**
THREAD:	left* overlock needle: decorative thread
	upper looper: coordinating thread if using 3-thread; no thread if using 2-thread
	lower looper: coordinating thread
KNIFE/CUTTER:	disengaged/non-cutting
DIFFERENTIAL FEED:	1 or "N"
ATTACHMENTS:	blind hem foot, very helpful
TENSIONS:	flatlock, 2 or 3-thread; if you cannot get the needle tension loose enough with thicker threads, take the thread completely out of the tension disc
LENGTH:	1-4, depending on weight of decorative threads and desired effect.

* Most 4-threads will use the left overlock needle for wide stitch; most 5-thread sergers will use the right (back) needle (if your 5-thread has two right (back) needle positions, use the most outside/left of this needle position). For questions, consult your instruction manual or local dealer.

** Check your instruction manual or local dealer to verify the use of regular sewing machine needle in your serger.

SUPPLIES

- project fabric
- 1 spool of decorative thread; choose from 30 wt. embroidery threads, metallic threads, or most medium weight decorative threads. See charts on pgs. 30 and 31
- 1-2 spools of thread to coordinate with fabric/decorative thread or invisible thread
- blind hem foot (optional, but very helpful)
- extras-optional, to add texture and design: *Designer Threads; Embellish Thread* cards; silk or *Spark Organdy* ribbons; charms; novelty shank buttons, etc.
- size 80/12 or 90/14 metallic needle (*Metafil, Metalfil, Metallic, Metallica*)

FABRIC PREPARATION

1. Preshrink, dry and press all fabrics.
2. Mark the reverse flatlock placement lines on the wrong side of the fabric using a wash out pencil.

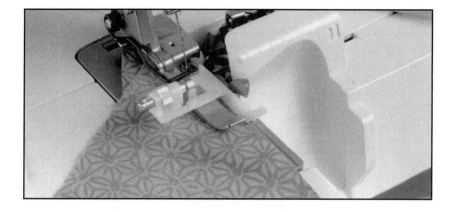

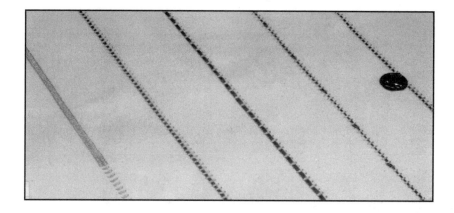

1. Fold the fabric on the marked line, right sides together. Press a crease on the fold.

2. Serge along the fold, allowing some of the loops to hang off the folded edge so the flatlock will lay flat when pulled apart. Pull the strip flat and finger press. The ladder will be on the right side.

Helpful Hint:
Using a scrap of the same fabric, if available, practice not only the tensions but where to guide the fabric fold as you serge. The use of a blind hem foot on some sergers can aid in guiding the fold consistently. Adjust the blind hem foot guide as you practice until the right amount of loops hang off the edge to allow the fold to pull open flat.

3. Press the fabric flat/smooth from the wrong side. If using heat-sensitive threads, use a press cloth to prevent melting or shrinking.

4. OPTIONAL- There are various ways you can add more creativity to your reverse flatlock, including:
   A. Shorten the stitch length to give a more satin-like appearance.
   B. Plain weave a novelty yarn/cord, or *Ribbon Thread*, in and out of the ladder "bars" of the stitch.
   C. Vary the weaving method; over 2, under 2; over 1, under 2; over 2, under 1; etc.
   D. As you are weaving, tie knots in the novelty thread/cord and adjust the position of the knot to lay on the top of the ladder bars.
   E. Weave or tie charms or beads to the thread/cord and adjust the position of the item to lay on the top of the ladder bars.

Cross-Woven Reverse Flatlock

Cross-Woven reverse flatlock is a variation of the reverse flatlock. After the thicker "ladder" bars are stitched, a wide flat ribbon or braid is woven in and out twice to create the desired effect.

SUPPLIES

- project fabric
- 1 spool of decorative thread (recommend the use of 30 wt. embroidery thread, metallic threads or *Designer 6/Decor 6* for best results)
- 1-2 cones of thread to coordinate
- flat ribbon to weave with: *Ribbon Thread, Ribbon Floss,* 2mm silk ribbon or *Carat*
- 12/80 or 14/90 metallic needle *(Metafil, Metalfil, Metallic, Metallica)*
- blind hem foot, very helpful
- *Ribbon Weaver,* or *Tail Tucker*

FABRIC PREPARATION

1. Preshrink, dry and press all fabrics.
2. Mark the reverse flatlock placement lines on the wrong side of the fabric using a wash out pencil.

SERGER SET-UP:	2 or 3-Thread Flatlock
MACHINE SET-UP:	wide plate/stitch finger/foot; for 2-thread, use converter on upper looper; 12/80 or 14/90 metallic needle**
THREAD:	left* overlock needle: decorative thread
	upper looper: FOR 3-THREAD ONLY-coordinating thread
	lower looper: coordinating thread
KNIFE/CUTTER:	disengaged/non-cutting
DIFFERENTIAL FEED:	1 or "N" (depending on fabric and area sewing)
ATTACHMENTS:	blind hem foot (optional, but very helpful)
TENSIONS:	flatlock, 2 or 3-thread
LENGTH:	4-5

* The needle you use will depend on your machine style. Most 4-threads will use the left overlock needle; most 5-thread sergers will use the right needle (if your 5-thread has two right (back) needle positions, use the most outside/left of this position.)

**Check your instruction manual or local dealer, to verify you can use machine needles in your serger.

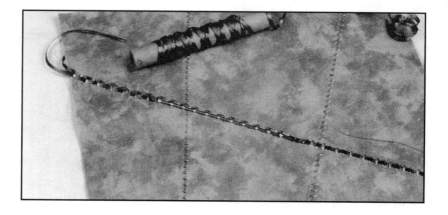

1. Fold the fabric on the marked line, right sides together. Press a crease on the fold.

2. Serge along the fold, allowing some of the loops to hang off the folded edge so the flatlock will lay flat when pulled open.

3. Pull the seam flat and finger press. The decorative "ladder" should be on the right side. Press the fabric flat/smooth, from the wrong side to protect the decorative threads.

4. Press *Ribbon Thread, Ribbon Floss* or 2mm silk ribbon flat. This will help eliminate the curling as you weave. DO NOT press metallic *Ribbon Thread* or *Carat* because it might melt.

5. Thread a *Ribbon Weaver,* or *Tail Tucker,* with the flat ribbon braid. Weave the ribbon over and under the "ladder" bars on the right side of your fabric. At the end of the seam, weave in the reverse direction. When reverse weaving, the ribbon thread should weave over and under the opposite bars from the first row. See photo.

Helpful Hint:
Using a scrap of the same fabric, if available, practice not only the tensions but where to guide the fabric fold as you serge. The use of a blind hem foot on some sergers can aid in guiding the fold consistently. Adjust the blind hem foot guide as you practice until the right amount of loops hang off the edge to allow the fold to pull open flat.

Ribbon Faggoting

What a great combination... flatlock and ribbon. There are all sorts of wonderful ribbons available today, so why not serge them together with decorative flatlock and create a new fabric!

SUPPLIES:

- ⅝" or wider ribbon (satin ribbon does not seem to hold up as well as other types of ribbon)
- ⅛"-¼" ribbon for weaving
- 1 spool of decorative thread; (recommend the use of 30 wt. embroidery thread, metallic threads or *Designer 6/Decor 6* for best results)
- 1-2 spools/cones of thread to coordinate
- 12/80 or 14/90 metallic needle (*Metafil, Metalfil, Metallic, Metallica*)
- large eye needle or *Tail Tucker*
- serger blind hem foot, very helpful

SERGER SET-UP:	*2 or 3-Thread Flatlock*
MACHINE SET-UP:	wide plate/stitch finger/foot; 2-thread converter on upper looper (for 2-thread flatlock only); 80/12 or 90/14 metallic needle **
THREAD:	left overlock needle*: decorative thread (see supply list for suggestions)
	upper looper: 2-thread converter (for 2-thread flatlock only) and no thread; coordinating thread (for 3-thread flatlock)
	lower looper: coordinating thread
KNIFE/CUTTER:	disengaged/non-cutting
DIFFERENTIAL FEED:	1 or "N"
ATTACHMENTS:	blind hem foot (optional, but very helpful)
TENSIONS:	flatlock, 2 or 3-thread
LENGTH:	4-5

*Most 4-thread sergers will use the left overlock needle; most 5-thread sergers will use the outside, right (back) needle position. For questions, consult your instruction manual or with your local dealer.

**Check your instruction manual or local dealer to verify if you can use regular sewing machine needles in your serger.

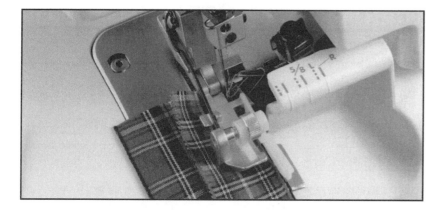 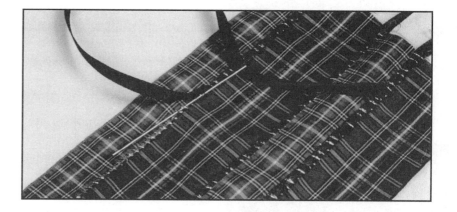

1. Adjust the guide on the blind hem foot to be very close to the overlock needle.

> **Helpful Hint:**
> **Some blind hem feet do not allow you to sew with the left overlock needle. If the blind hem foot cannot be used, use the regular presser foot, serge slowly, and guide the ribbon as described.**

2. Stack 2 pieces of wide ribbon, right sides together with right edge even. Place on the serger, with the edge of the ribbons against the blind hem foot guide.

3. Serge so the needle just barely catches the two ribbon edges. Thread loops will hang off the ribbon edge. Keep the ribbon edges against the adjustable guide. The closer to the edge and the more the loops hangs off the edge, the wider the space between the ribbons will be (wider faggoting).

4. Pull ribbons open and apart to create the open faggoting look.

5. Continue adding more and more ribbons together following steps 2-4, until desired fabric width is reached.

6. Thread the narrow ribbon through a large eye needle or *Tail Tucker*. Weave in and out of the flatlock bars to finish.

Serger Seminole

Serger Seminole is a stylistic modification of Seminole Patchwork. The following are general guidelines for a basic style of seminole. They are intended as guidelines only and can be adjusted to meet your specific needs.

This chapter will introduce you to a basic Seminole patchwork design. If you like this style of piecing, consult a book on Seminole Patchwork and modify it – serger style.

SUPPLIES

- fabric as follows*:
  center (A) – ⅛ yd (1-1/2" used)
  second (B) – ⅛ yd (3" used)
  third (C) – ⅛ yd (4" used)
  border – ⅛ yd (2-½" used)**
- 2 spools of decorative thread, these can be the same or different; at least one spool has to be light enough to be used for a rolled/narrow hem.
- regular thread to coordinate with decorative thread(s)
- machine Quilting needle
- rotary cutter, mat and ruler
- invisible thread
- sewing machine
- blind hem foot or seam guide; optional, but very helpful

*SIZE: the finished band will be approximately 30-35" long. If a longer band is needed, you may need to purchase more fabric yardage and double the strip requirements.

**NOTE: The border yardage is approximate based on suggested width. Use color A, color B or new color for border.

FABRIC PREPARATION

1. Pre-shrink and press all fabrics.
2. Cut strips as follows using rotary cutting equipment:
   - 1 strip of center color A 1½" wide by fabric width
   - 2 strips of color B 1½" wide by fabric width
   - 2 strips of color C 2" wide by fabric width
   - 2 strips of border 1¼" wide by fabric width

2 or 3-Thread Flatlock

MACHINE SET-UP: left overlock needle; wide plate/stitch finger/foot; 2-thread converter (if using 2-thread flatlock); Quilting needle**

THREAD: left* overlock needle: thread to match fabric or coordinate with decorative thread.

upper looper: for 3-thread your choice of decorative thread(s); for 2-thread, no thread.

lower looper: for 3-thread, thread to coordinate with decorative thread; for 2-thread, your choice of decorative thread

KNIFE/CUTTER: engaged/cutting

DIFFERENTIAL FEED: 1, or as needed for fabric

ATTACHMENTS: seam guide or blind hem foot helpful

TENSIONS: flatlock, 2 or 3-thread

LENGTH: varies by weight of decorative thread and desired effect

* Some 4-thread sergers will not stitch with just the left overlock needle. If you own this kind of serger, use the right overlock needle.

** Not all sergers can use sewing machine needles, check your instruction manual or dealer.

1. Serge strips, **wrong sides** together, along the lengthwise edges. Serge in the following order: C-B-A-B-C. It is very important to keep the seam allowances consistent or the seams will not match later. Using a seam guide or blind hem foot will help keep the seam allowances consistent. Use the cutter as you serge to cut off the "fuzzies" but no real fabric. Pull open each seam after serged.

Design note:
Create a narrower band by using strips: C-A-C.
Eliminate color B and cut C the same width as indicated.

Serger Seminole *(cont.)*

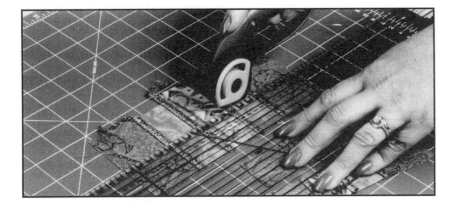

3. Press smooth from the wrong side of the strips.

4. Using a rotary cutter, cut the strips even along one end and/or remove selvages along one end. Cross cut the remaining stripped fabric into 1½" strips.

SERGER SET-UP:	*2 or 3-Thread Narrow or Rolled Hem*
MACHINE SET-UP:	right* overlock needle; narrow plate/stitch finger; 2-thread converter (if using 2-thread rolled hem); fixed cutter adjustments if needed
THREAD:	right* overlock needle: thread to match fabric or coordinate with decorative thread. upper looper: for 3-thread, your choice of decorative thread(s); for 2-thread, use the two thread converter and no thread lower looper: for 3-thread, thread to match fabric or coordinate with decorative thread(s); for 2-thread, your choice of decorative thread
KNIFE/CUTTER:	engaged/cutting
DIFFERENTIAL FEED:	1 (depends on fabric)
ATTACHMENTS:	none
TENSIONS:	rolled hem, 2 or 3 thread; or 3-thread narrow hem
LENGTH:	varies by weight of decorative thread and desired effect

*Some 4-thread serger models require the use of the left overlock needle for rolled and narrow hems. Please check your owner's manual or with your local dealer if you have any questions.

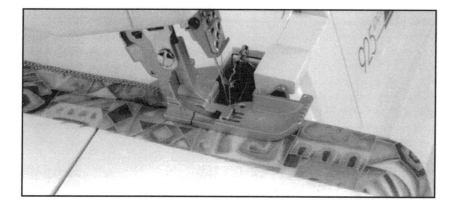

5. Set up serger for 3-thread narrow hem, or rolled hem, for finishing border strips (see box at **left**).

6. Serge/roll hem on one lengthwise edge of the border strip. Guide the fabric so the "fuzzies" are removed, but no real fabric is cut off.

7. Set-up serger for piecing strips together and attaching borders (see box at right).

SERGER SET-UP:	*Piecing Strips/Attaching Borders*
MACHINE SET-UP:	2-thread chain or 3,4 or 5-thread; ¼" seam if possible; Quilting needle*
THREAD:	all positions use regular or cone thread to match fabrics
KNIFE/CUTTER:	engaged/cutting
DIFFERENTIAL FEED:	1 (may depend on fabric)
ATTACHMENTS:	seam guide or blind hem foot, optional, but very helpful
TENSIONS:	normal
LENGTH:	2

* Not all sergers will allow the use of sewing machine needles, check with your instruction manual or dealer if you have any questions.

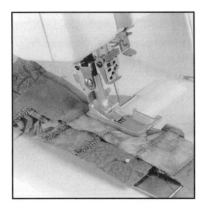

8. Serge new pieced strips right sides together. As you sew, match up the seams by shifting the raw edges down by one square. Can complete this step by sewing machine if desired. Serge or sew the seam with a ¼" seam allowance.

Design Note:
Either match the decorative flatlock exactly in a line or off set the squares by the width of the stitching.

9. Press all seams in the same direction. Use a press cloth on the right side to protect decorative threads.

10. With the pieced band face up, cut the zig zag edges even by cutting off the triangles along both edges. Use a rotary cutter, mat and ruler.

11. Serge border strip to the pieced band, right sides together. Match the newly cut edge to the unfinished border edge. Use ¼" seams.

PROJECT APPLICATION

1. Set up sewing machine (see box at left).

2. Place the Seminole strip with the border in the desired position on your project, right side up. Pin in place. Stitch the strips into place by straight stitching along the decorative hem/edge, "in the ditch". Stitching right next to the narrow edge will make the heavy edge stand up resembling a small piping in the seam.

Striking Strips

This effect is really a sampler of many different techniques employing a variety of different decorative threads. It is a great way to familiarize yourself with many stitch types and threads while creating a novelty piece of fabric.

The best stitches for assembling the strips are: flatlock, rolled hem, reverse flatlock and cover hem. Special instructions for the use of these stitches to assemble the strips are included in this section.

SUPPLIES

- fashion fabrics, at least 2-3 coordinated fabrics for interest
- a variety of light, medium, and heavy weight decorative threads (see thread charts on pages 30 and 31 for ideas on which threads work best in each looper) coordinated with fabrics
- novelty threads to add texture
- 1-2 spools of regular thread to coordinate with the decorative threads
- glasshead pins
- rotary cutter, mat, ruler
- blind hem foot (optional)

FABRIC PREPARATION

1. Preshrink and press all fabrics.
2. Cut fabrics into strips of various widths ranging from 1" to 3" using a rotary cutter, mat and ruler. The desired length of a piece of finished fabric will determine the amount of strips needed. Strips can be cut in half and used, if the fabric piece desired is no more than 22" wide.
3. Lay out your strips in the order you want them serged. Here is a diagram as an example to get you started.

fabric A	1"
fabric B	1-3/4"
fabric C	2-1/2"
fabric B	1-1/4"
fabric C	1-3/4"
fabric B	1-1/4"
fabric A	3"
fabric B	1-1/2"

1. Decide which techniques and threads you are going to use for each seam. Here's an example, labeled with stitch types.

Follow steps 2-4 for flatlock, reverse flatlock and rolled hem seams. Follow step 5 for cover hem seams.

If fabrics are very soft, you may need to use spray starch or a spray stabilizer for added body.

Find the general machine set-up for all the different stitch types in section titled *"What Tensions Should Look Like"*, starting on page 16

flatlock

rolled hem

reverse flatlock

rolled hem

cover hem

flatlock

rolled hem

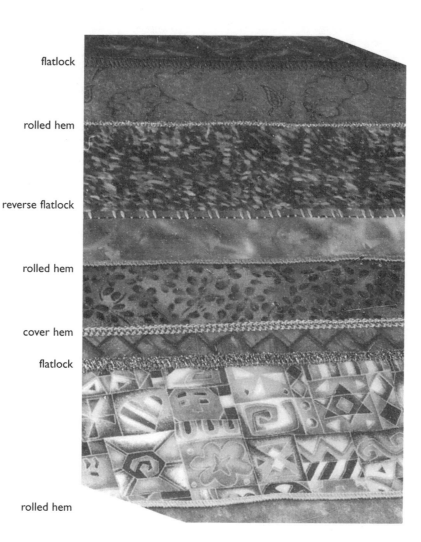

2. Stack the first two strips with the seam edges even. If using **rolled hem** or **flatlock** place them **wrong** sides together. If using **reverse flatlock** place **right** sides together.

3. Serge. Open the strips out and press seam smooth, or to one side for rolled hem. Use a pressing cloth over the decorative thread to protect it from the heat.

Striking Strips *(cont.)*

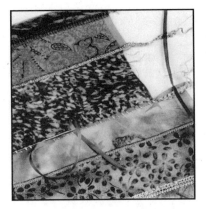
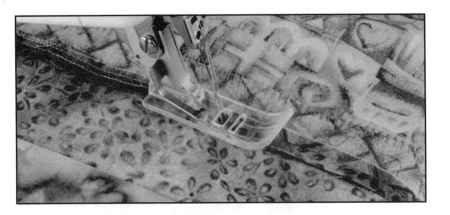

4. Weave novelty yarns or threads in reverse flatlocking if desired. See Novelty Reverse Flatlocking section for ideas.

5. FOR COVER HEM ONLY: Stitch a ¼" seam right sides together with the sewing machine. Press the seam allowance open. Place sewn seam under the serger presser foot, seam allowance up and fabric right side against the serger. Stitch, centering over the previously sewn seam. Press from wrong side, if needed.

6. Repeat steps 2-5 as needed.

7. After the fabric is constructed, pin the pattern piece in place. Dot seam sealant along the edge of the pattern at the strip seam lines where they will be cut. Let dry completely.

8. Cut out pattern piece and construct project.

Striking Strips
Serger Seminole
Single Color Serger Points
Flatlock Fringe
Pick-Up Sticks
Charming Chains
Novelty Reverse Flatlock

Squared Bisquits, Kite Tails,
Decorative Cover Hem,
Middy Braid, Chain Stitch

Pick-Up Sticks
Curly Ringlets
Wavy Lattice

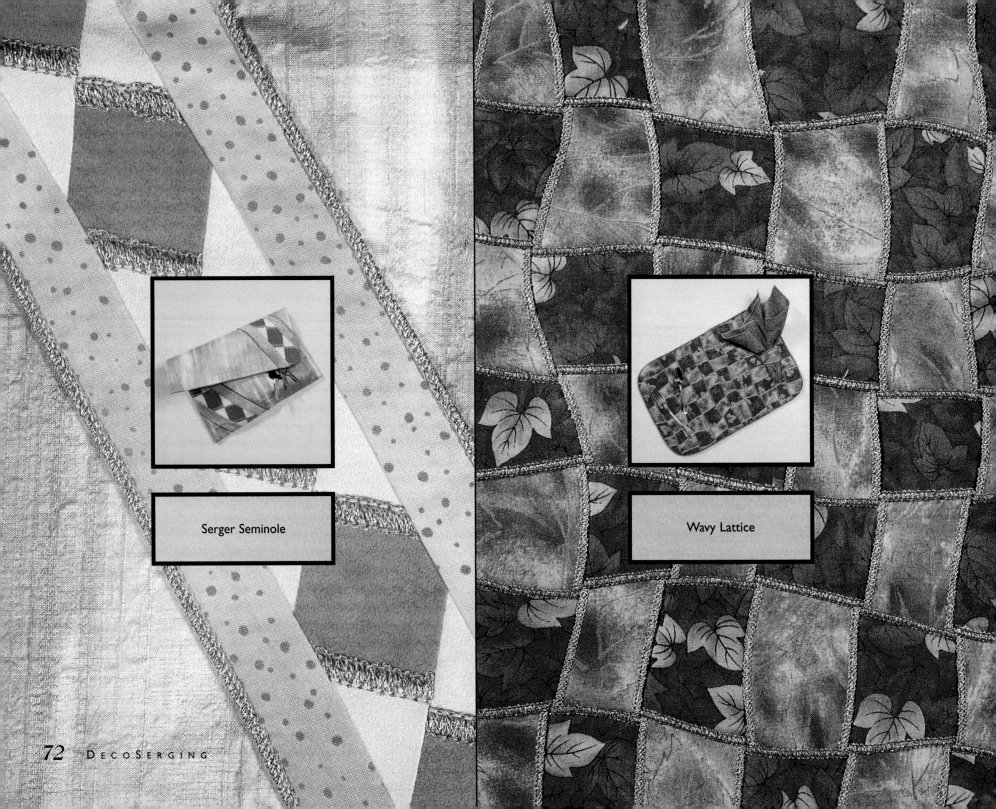

Serger Seminole

Wavy Lattice

Cross Woven Reverse Flatlock
Single Color Tabs

Serger Lattice

Serger Seminole
Decorative Rolled Hem

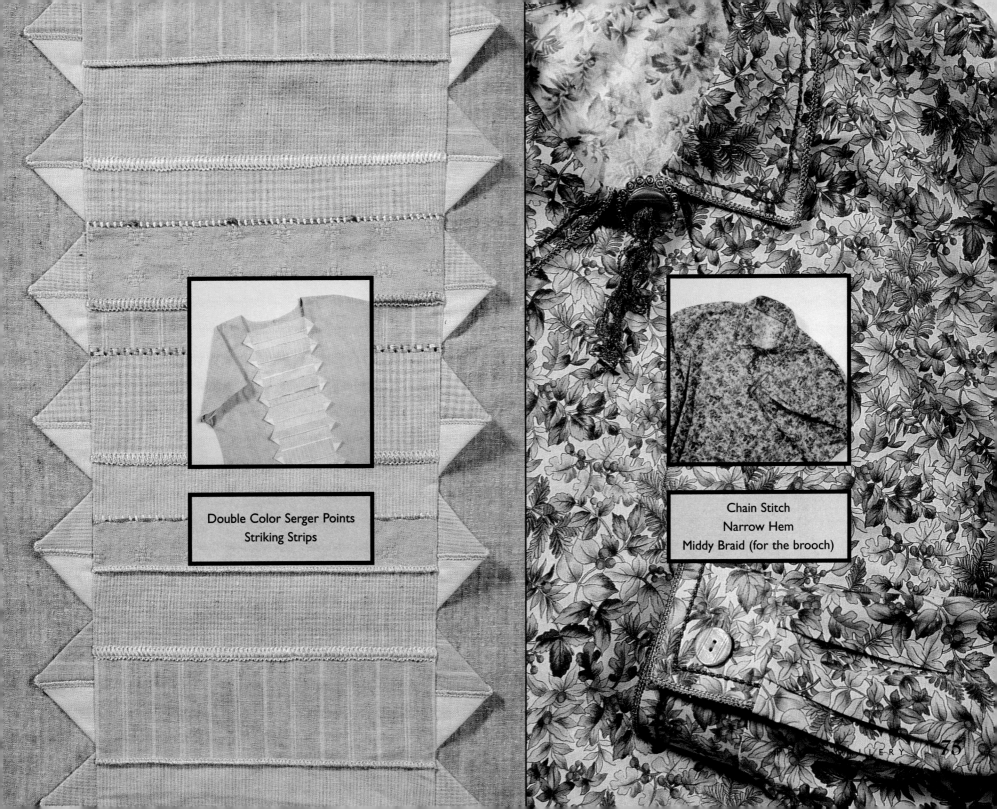

Double Color Serger Points
Striking Strips

Chain Stitch
Narrow Hem
Middy Braid (for the brooch)

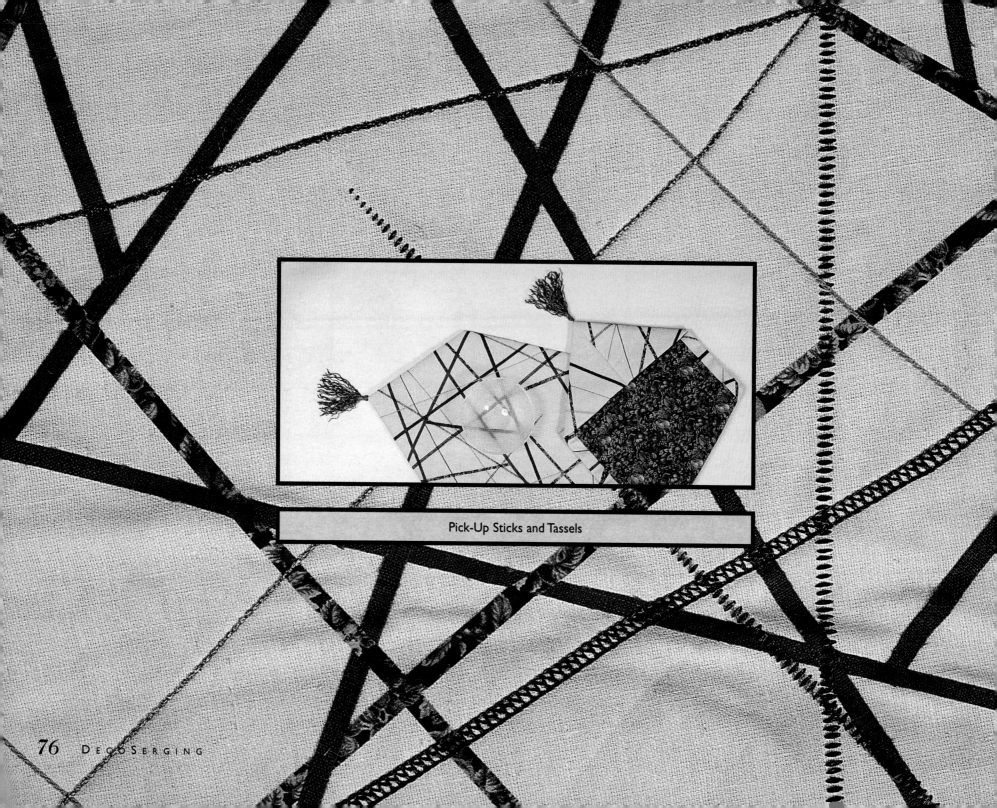

Pick-Up Sticks and Tassels

Ribbon Faggoting

Middy Braid
Rolled Hem Pintucks

Novelty Reverse Flatlock
Serger Soutache
Flatlock and Tassel

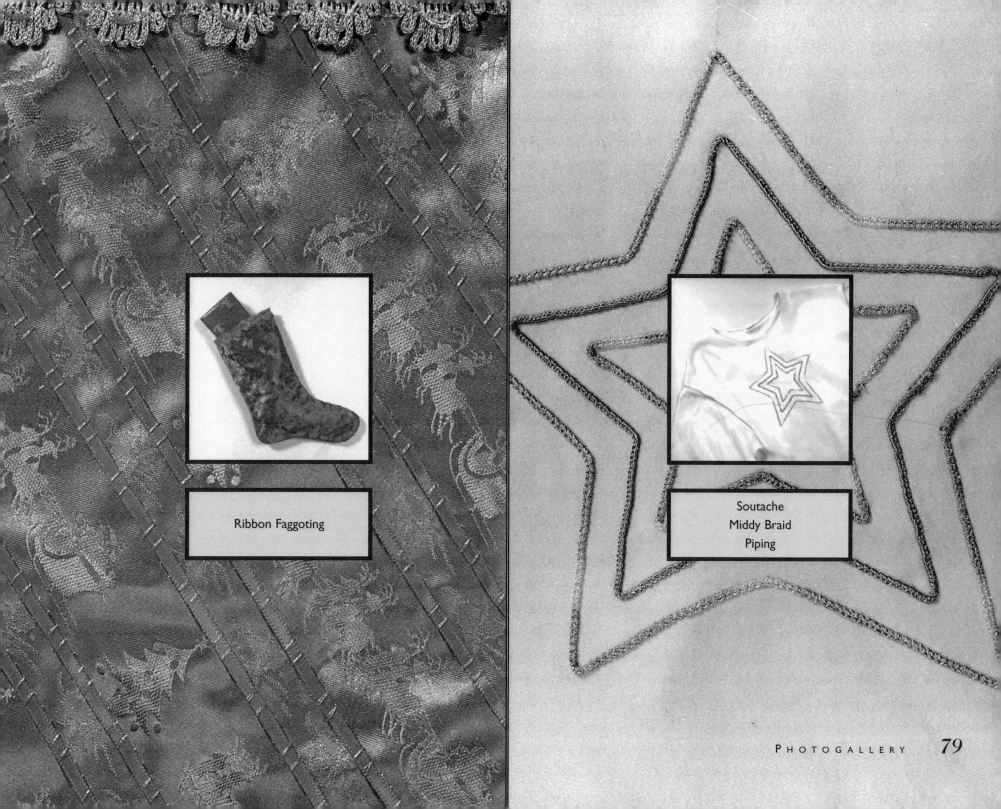

Ribbon Faggoting

Soutache
Middy Braid
Piping

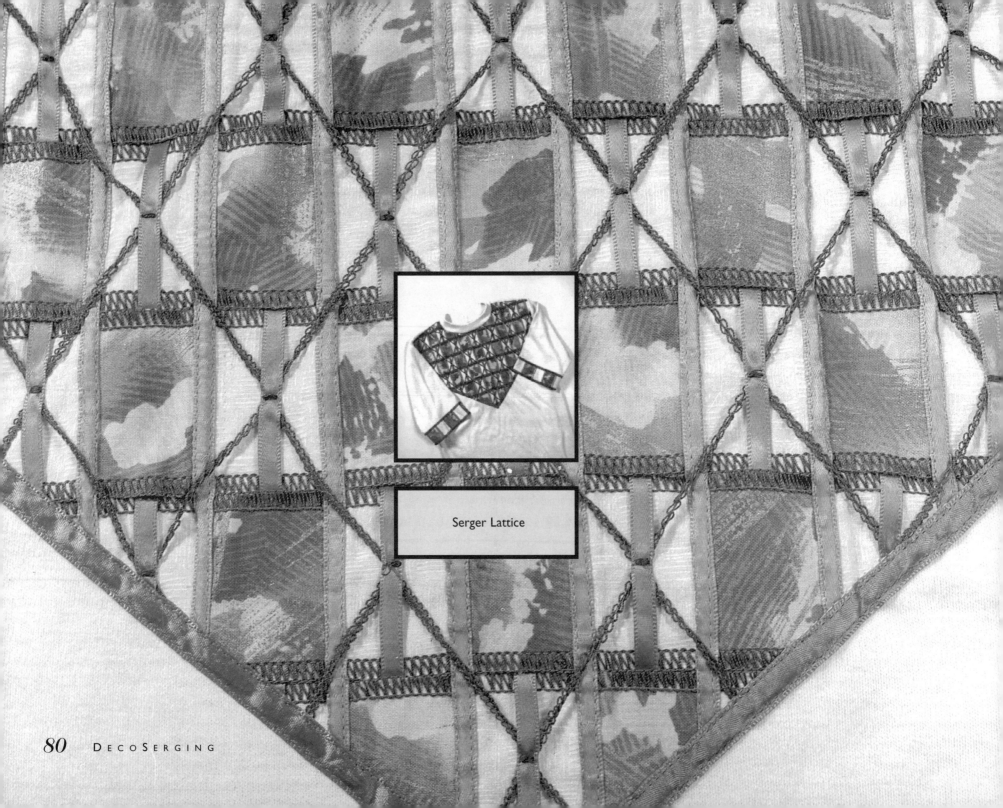

Serger Lattice

Serger Lattice

This technique combines a decorative serging stitch, the sewing machine, and various directional weaving pieces to create a very interesting, textured piece of "fabric".

The new "fabric" is made for each pattern piece needed, so there is very little "fabric" wasted. This is not the fastest technique, but well worth the effect.

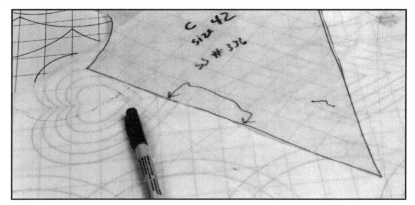

FABRIC PREPARATION

1. Preshrink, dry, and press all fabrics.
2. Cut main and coordinating fabric into 2" strips, crossgrain. Use a rotary cutter, mat and ruler.
3. Trace the pattern piece on the **wrong** (fusible) side of the iron-on interfacing, using a permanent marker.
4. Draw a horizontal and vertical grain lines from seam line to seam line in the center of the pattern piece.
5. Place the interfacing on the pinning board or pressing board, fusible side up.

SUPPLIES

- main fabric and coordinating fabric
- ¼" ribbon in 1-3 colors
- 2-3 spools of medium weight decorative thread (see Decorative Thread Library charts, pgs. 30 and 31, for suggestions)
- 2 spools of matching thread for each color ribbon
- serger thread to match fabric
- 2 spools of regular thread to coordinate with decorative thread
- twin needle, size 3.0 or 4.0
- size 80/12 Universal needle
- light weight fusible interfacing, slightly larger than pattern piece size
- weaving/pressing board (can use ironing board if large enough)
- glasshead straight pins
- *Tail Tucker*
- permanent marker
- non-stick (appliqué) pressing sheet
- rotary cutter, mat, ruler

Serger Lattice *(cont.)*

SERGER SET-UP:	*Seaming*
MACHINE SET-UP:	¼" seam, with 3, 4, 5 thread or chain stitch
THREAD:	all positions: cone or spool thread to match fabrics
KNIFE/CUTTER:	engaged/cutting
DIFFERENTIAL FEED:	1 or "N" normal
ATTACHMENTS:	none or seam guide
TENSIONS:	"normal" for stitch chosen
LENGTH:	2.5

1. Serge strips of main fabric and coordinating fabric together along the long edges, right sides together. Do not allow the serger to cut off any fabric, except the "fuzzy" edges. Alternate the two fabrics and continue to sew strips together until the width of the strips measures a bit wider than the width or length of the pattern piece (yoke, pillow top, vest front, etc.).

2. Press all seams in one direction.

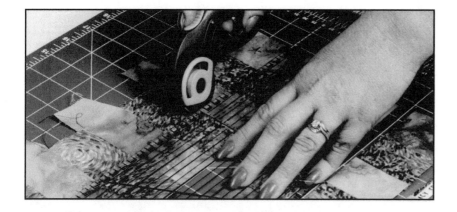

3. Lay serged strips on the cutting mat and line them up with the printed grid. Cut one edge even. Cross-cut into 2" strips across the newly formed fabric. Adjust the cutting edge after every few cuts so that the strips remain straight.

4. Set-up serger for 3-Thread Decorative Edge (see box at right). Serge along both of the long edges of the new strips. Do not be too concerned if the edge looks different at the seam lines. This will not show after the ribbon is applied.

SERGER SET-UP:	3-Thread Decorative Edge
MACHINE SET-UP:	use the stitch finger/plate/foot and needle position to create a medium width serged edge
THREAD:	overlock needle: thread to match decorative thread
	upper looper: novelty decorative thread
	lower looper: thread to match decorative thread
KNIFE/CUTTER:	engaged/cutting
DIFFERENTIAL FEED:	1 or "N" normal, or as needed
ATTACHMENTS:	none
TENSIONS:	"normal" balanced edge
LENGTH:	varies by weight of thread and desired effect

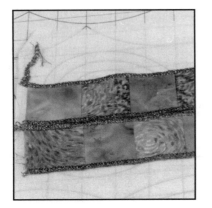

5. Position the serged strips right side up on fusible side of the interfacing. Start the first strip out on the vertical or horizontal drawn line. Place the second strip next to the first, slide the strip so the fabrics alternate, matching seam lines as much as possible. Continue to lay the strips side by side, **without** overlapping them, until the pattern piece is more than completely covered.

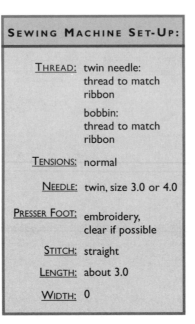

SEWING MACHINE SET-UP:	
THREAD:	twin needle: thread to match ribbon
	bobbin: thread to match ribbon
TENSIONS:	normal
NEEDLE:	twin, size 3.0 or 4.0
PRESSER FOOT:	embroidery, clear if possible
STITCH:	straight
LENGTH:	about 3.0
WIDTH:	0

6. Press with the tip or side of the iron, at the seam lines **only**, to adhere the fabric strips to the interfacing.

7. Set the sewing machine as specified above.

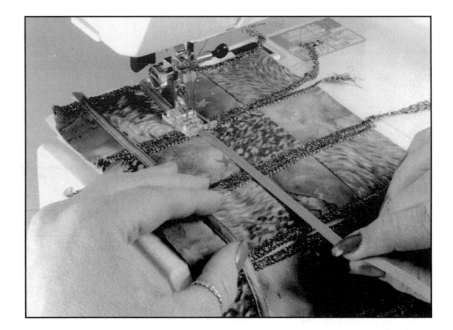

8. Center ribbon (or ribbons if using different colors) over the seam lines of the strips and pin. Let extra ribbon overlap the edge of the strips. Pin in place.

9. Machine stitch the ribbon in place. Keep the twin needle stitching centered on the ribbon.

10. Weave the remaining ribbon color in and out of the loosely serged strips. Alternate weaving in each row, so you will always weave over and under the same fabric print.

11. Fuse all ribbon and strips to the interfacing.

SERGER SET-UP:	*2 or 3-Thread Rolled Hem*
MACHINE SET-UP:	right* overlock needle; a rolled hem plate/stitch finger/foot; 2-thread converter (for 2-thread rolled hem only); fixed cutter adjustment as machine manual instructs
THREAD:	right* overlock needle: matching or coordinating thread
	upper looper: light or medium weight decorative thread if using 3-thread rolled hem; no thread if using 2-thread rolled hem
	lower looper: coordinating thread if using 3-thread rolled hem; decorative thread if using 2-thread rolled hem
KNIFE/CUTTER:	disengaged/non-cutting
DIFFERENTIAL FEED:	0.5 - 1, depends on fabric
ATTACHMENTS:	none
TENSIONS:	2 or 3-thread rolled hem
LENGTH:	1.0 to 1.5, depending on the decorative thread used

* There are a few serger models that require the use of the left overlock needle for a rolled hem, not the right. If you have any questions consult your instruction manual (see: rolled hem) or your local dealer.

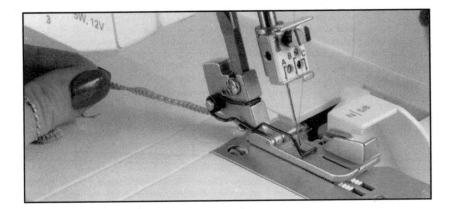

12. Set up the serger for 2 or 3-thread rolled hem (see box on previous page). Test the tensions on scrap fabric to help make any adjustments needed.

13. Without fabric, serge. As the serger creates decorative chain, hold the chain taut straight back and slightly to the left to feed off the stitch finger. Serge off the amount of decorative chain needed. If the chain looks like there are skipped stitches or holes in it, you are probably pulling the chain off the stitch finger too fast. It helps to set the serger speed at a rate you can control. If you have some yardage with these holes don't fear, we will be cutting this chain so those bad spots can be cut out.

14. Thread the chain on the *Tail Tucker*. Weave the chain diagonally in and out of the loose woven ribbon. First weave all in one diagonal direction, then weave in the opposite direction. See photo. Secure the ends on the interfacing by first pinning, then pressing with the tip of an iron. Be careful not to stretch the chains or leave them too loose as you weave.

15. Set the sewing machine as specified above.

16. Hold decorative chains in place by stitching them with a bar tack where they cross over.

17. Press finished fabric piece from the front with pressing cloth (to protect decorative threads) and then again from the wrong side. When pressing from the wrong side, be careful not to press the interfacing to the pressing surface. The use of a non-stick pressing sheet (appliqué sheet) will prevent this when using any fusible. Your "fabric" is now complete.

18. Lay pattern piece on the new fabric. You may want to baste down loose ribbons and chain in the seam allowance of piece before cutting out pattern.

Wavy Lattice

This is a very easy woven technique. It creates a unique piece of fabric that is suitable for home decor or garment projects. As with many techniques, you will recreate a piece of fabric and then cut out the pattern piece(s) needed.

SUPPLIES

- main fabric
  - for yardage amount, measure the finished desired fabric width, plus a little extra
- coordinating fabric –
  for yardage amount, measure the finished length of fabric needed, plus a little extra
- light weight fusible interfacing, piece slightly larger than needed; the interfacing can be pieced, if needed
- extra fusible knit interfacing (if your main and/or coordinating fabric(s) are very light weight)
- 1-2 spools of light or medium weight decorative thread; you can mix threads to create your own, too
- 2 spools of regular thread to coordinate for each color of decorative thread
- weaving/pressing board (can use ironing board if large enough), very helpful, but not absolutely needed
- rotary cutter and mat
- glasshead pins
- non-stick (appliqué) pressing sheet

FABRIC PREPARATION

1. Preshrink and dry all fabrics and interfacings. Press fabrics, if needed.

2. OPTIONAL: Fuse light weight, knit interfacing to the wrong side of the fabrics if needed for added body.

3. Place main fabric on cutting mat. Using a rotary cutter, cut random width wavy strips from selvage to selvage. Be kind to yourself, do not cut the curves too deep. Carefully remove the wavy strips, **in order,** from the mat and set aside.

4. Repeat step 3 using the coordinating fabric.

5. Place the interfacing, fusible side up, on the pinning/pressing surface.

SERGER SET-UP:	*Narrow Hem*
MACHINE SET-UP:	narrow stitch plate/finger/foot; adjust fixed cutter as manual indicates
THREAD:	right* overlock needle: thread to coordinate with the decorative thread or fabric
	upper looper: light weight or medium weight decorative thread
	lower looper: thread to coordinate with the decorative thread or fabric
KNIFE/CUTTER:	engaged/cutting
DIFFERENTIAL FEED:	1 or "N"
ATTACHMENTS:	none
TENSIONS:	3-thread narrow hem/edge
LENGTH:	1-2, depending on threads and desired effect.

*There are models that use left overlock needle for a rolled hem. If you have any questions, consult your instruction manual or your local dealer.

Wavy Lattice *(cont.)*

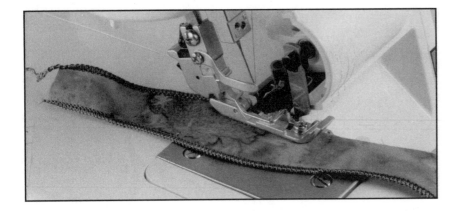

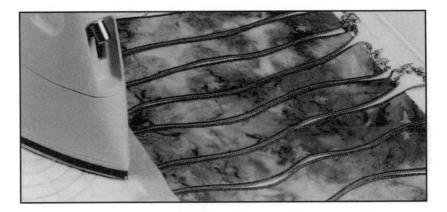

1. With right side up, serge along both long, wavy edges of the main fabric strips. Do not cut off any fabric from the edge. Carefully keep the strips in the order they were cut, otherwise it becomes a difficult puzzle to fit back together.

2. Repeat step 1 for the coordinating fabric.

3. Place the serged, main fabric strips on the interfacing in order. Align the fabric selvage with the side (vertical) edge of the interfacing. Pin if needed.

4. Press the strips in place along the selvage, one inch down. DO NOT press any further into the fabric. Use a non-stick (appliqué) pressing sheet to protect the iron's heating sole from the interfacing.

5. Take the first coordinating strip and weave it vertically, in and out of the main fabric strips. Align the fabric selvage to the top edge (horizontal) of the interfacing. Pin if needed.

6. Press into place along the selvage edge, no more than one inch down.

7. Weave the second coordinating strip next to the first strip. Slide the fabric edges as close together as possible. Be sure to weave in and out the opposite of the first strip. Pin in place.

8. Press into place along the selvage edge.

9. Repeat steps 7 and 8 until all strips are woven.

10. Adjust strips as needed. With the use of a non-stick pressing sheet, fuse/press all the strips in place. Turn the piece over and press from the interfacing side to assure a complete fuse. If fabric allows, use steam or moisture with the second pressing.

Squared Bisquits

For this technique you will start with a fabric square that has been decoratively serged. This square is then folded to form a unique 3-dimensional raised square in the center of the fabric square. They can be pieced into all sorts of projects and are especially fun mixed with other squares of flat fabric.

SUPPLIES

- fashion fabric(s)*
- muslin or left over fabric for base
- 1 or more spools of decorative threads; the weight and type to be determined by the type of decorative stitching you choose, refer to Decorative Thread Library Charts, pgs. 30 and 31
- 1-2 spools of thread to coordinate with fabric/decorative threads
- serger accessories (recommended); clear chain stitch foot, clear cover hem foot, blind hem foot
- glasshead straight pins
- rotary cutter, mat, ruler
- sewing machine
- 80/12 or 90/14 metallic needle (*Metafil, Metallica, Metallic, Metalfil*) if planning reverse flatlock

FABRIC PREPARATION

1. Preshrink, dry and press all fabrics.
2. Cut 3" x 3" squares of muslin or other base fabric. Cut 4" x 4" squares of fashion fabric. This base square size can vary, by how big or small you want the formed, center square. The size of the finished square will be ½" smaller than the cut measurements of the base square.
3. Using a washout pencil, draw a line down the center of each fashion fabric square. Draw the line on the **right** side if you plan to flatlock. Draw the line on the **wrong** side if you plan to reverse flatlock, chainstitch or cover hem.

*Design Note: You can use a single fabric or several fabrics for added interest.

1. Decorate the right side, on the marked line of the fashion fabric squares using the chain stitch, cover hem, flatlock or reverse flatlock. Use the following boxes for specifics of each stitch type. Fold the fabric as indicated.

SERGER SET-UP:	*Decorative Chain Stitch*
MACHINE SET-UP:	drop upper looper; attach flat sewing surface; etc. see instruction manual for specifics
THREAD:	chain needle: thread to coordinate
	chain looper: decorative thread—see thread charts on pgs. 30 and 31 for thread suggestions
KNIFE/CUTTER:	disengaged/non-cutting
DIFFERENTIAL FEED:	1 or "N"; normal
ATTACHMENTS:	possible clear chain stitch foot or regular foot
TENSIONS:	adjust for normal balanced chain stitch
LENGTH:	2.5 depending on weight of decorative threads and desired effect
FABRIC FOLD:	none
OTHER INSTRUCTIONS:	chain from the wrong side of the fabric, following the marked line

SERGER SET-UP:	*Decorative Cover Hem*
MACHINE SET-UP:	drop upper looper; attach flat sewing surface, etc. see instruction manual for specifics
THREAD:	cover hem needles: thread to coordinate
	cover hem looper: decorative thread—see thread charts on pgs. 30 and 31 for thread suggestions
KNIFE/CUTTER:	disengaged/non-cutting
DIFFERENTIAL FEED:	1 or "N"; normal
ATTACHMENTS:	possible clear cover hem foot or regular foot
TENSIONS:	adjust for "normal" LOOK of cover hem stitch
LENGTH:	2-4 depending on weight of decorative threads and desired effect
FABRIC FOLD:	none
OTHER INSTRUCTIONS:	stitch from the wrong side of the fabric, following the marked line

Squared Bisquits *(cont.)*

SERGER SET-UP:	*2 or 3-Thread Flatlock*
MACHINE SET-UP:	wide plate/stitch finger/foot; 2-thread converter on upper looper, if using 2-thread flatlock
THREAD:	left* overlock needle: thread to coordinate
	upper looper: decorative thread, if using 3-thread; no thread, using 2-thread
	lower looper: decorative thread, if using 2-thread; coordinating thread if using 3-thread
KNIFE/CUTTER:	disengaged/non-cutting
DIFFERENTIAL FEED:	1 or "N"; normal
ATTACHMENTS:	blind hem foot or regular foot
TENSIONS:	flatlock "LOOK"
LENGTH:	1 to 3, depending on weight of decorative threads and desired effect
FABRIC FOLD:	wrong sides together along marked line
OTHER INSTRUCTIONS:	serge along fabric fold letting enough looper threads hang off the edge for the fabric to lay flat; the use of a blind hem foot on some sergers will help guide the folded edge evenly, adjust as needed. Pull open and press from the wrong side when completed.

*Some 4-thread sergers will only do 3-thread with the right needle. Consult manual or local dealer if needed.

SERGER SET-UP:	*2 or 3-Thread Reverse Flatlock*
MACHINE SET-UP:	wide plate/stitch finger/foot; 2-thread converter on upper looper, if using 2-thread flatlock; size 80/12 needle or 90 Topstitch needle
THREAD:	left* overlock needle: decorative thread
	upper looper: serger thread, if using 3-thread; no thread, using 2-thread
	lower looper: coordinating thread if using 2 or 3-thread
KNIFE/CUTTER:	disengaged/non-cutting
DIFFERENTIAL FEED:	1 or "N"; normal
ATTACHMENTS:	blind hem foot or regular foot
TENSIONS:	flatlock "LOOK"
LENGTH:	1 to 4, depending on weight of decorative threads and desired effect
FABRIC FOLD:	right sides together along marked line
OTHER INSTRUCTIONS:	serge along fabric fold letting enough looper threads hang off the edge for the fabric to lay flat; the use of a blind hem foot on some sergers will help guide the folded edge evenly, adjust as needed. Pull open and press from the wrong side when completed. Weave other threads under the "bars" if desired. See Novelty Reverse Flatlock for specific weaving ideas.

*Some 4-thread sergers will only do 3-thread with the right needle. Consult manual or local dealer if needed.

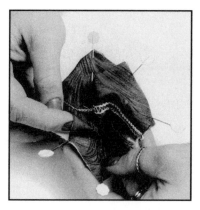 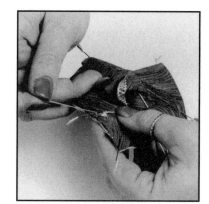  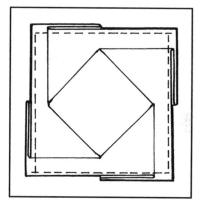

2. Fold all 3" base fabric squares in half, lengthwise and crosswise to determine the center of each side of the square. Mark these centers with a straight pin.

3. Lay larger fashion fabric square on top of smaller base square. Match corners of fashion fabric with base square and pin. Smooth the excess fashion fabric to the center from the right corner and pin.

4. Push the excess fabric over the center pin towards the corner forming a knife pleat. Pin pleat in place.

5. Repeat steps 3 and 4 for all sides of the square. All pleats must go in the **same** direction.

6. If you "twist" or manipulate the center of the biscuit, a decorated square will form and the puffiness will look more controlled.

7. Repeat step 4, 5 and 6 for all squares.

8. Using a serger or sewing machine, stitch ¼" from the raw edges of the pinned squares.

Design Note: You can vary the size of the base square or the fashion fabric as desired, but the fashion fabric square must be at least ½" larger than the base square. The size of the square formed in the center will change accordingly.

Pick-Up Sticks

This technique is very simple but has a fun effect. With the fused straight lines, it reminds me of the child's game, pick-up sticks, hence the name. After strips of coordinating fabric are fused in place, you will decoratively serge on the surface to keep the strips in place.

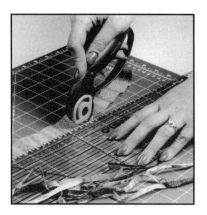

SUPPLIES

- foundation fabric (a little larger than the pattern piece you plan to cut from it)
- assorted coordinating fabrics
- light weight interfacing, or a tear away type stabilizer if base fabric is very light weight
- paper backed fusible webbing
- 1 or more spools of decorative threads; the weight and type to be determined by the type of decorative stitching you choose
- 1-3 spools/cones of thread to coordinate with fabric/decorative threads
- serger accessories (optional, but helpful): clear chain stitch foot, clear cover hem foot, blind hem foot
- seam sealant (*Fray Stop, No Fray, Fray Check*)
- rotary cutter, mat, ruler
- non-stick (appliqué) pressing sheet
- 80/12 metallic needle (*Metafil, Metalfil, Metallic, Metallica*) or 90/14 Topstitch needle if planning reverse flatlock

FABRIC PREPARATION

1. Preshrink, dry and press all fabrics.
2. Fuse the paper backed webbing to the wrong side of the assorted fabrics. Allow to cool completely.
3. Peel the paper backing off the assorted strips.
4. Using rotary cutting equipment, cut the assorted fabrics into ⅛" and ¼" strips.

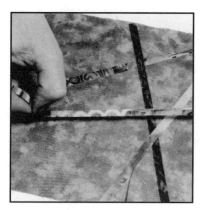

1. Position the assorted strips in a random manner on the foundation fabric. Overlapping the strips will create more interest. Do not overdo the "sticks" because you will still add stitching. The end result should be a random arrangement of sticks.

2. Using a non-stick pressing sheet, fuse the strips in place.

3. Fuse interfacing to the wrong side of foundation fabric, if needed. Pin stabilizer to the wrong side of foundation fabric, if needed.

4. To further decorate the piece of fabric and help secure fabric strips, use the following types of serger stitches. Any special instructions required will be provided with the stitch. Stitch in straight lines to keep with the pick-up sticks theme. Do not overdo the stitching.

SERGER SET-UP:	*Decorative Chain Stitch*
MACHINE SET-UP:	drop upper looper; attach flat sewing surface; etc. see instructional manual for specifics
THREAD:	chain needle: thread to coordinate
	chain looper: decorative thread – see thread charts on pgs. 30 and 31 for threads that work best
KNIFE/CUTTER:	disengaged/non-cutting
DIFFERENTIAL FEED:	1 or "N"; normal
ATTACHMENTS:	possible clear chain stitch foot or regular foot
TENSIONS:	adjust to get "normal" balanced chain stitch
LENGTH:	3 to 4, depending on weight of decorative threads and desired effect
OTHER INSTRUCTIONS:	stitch from the wrong side of the fabric

Pick-up Sticks *(cont.)*

SERGER SET-UP: *Decorative Cover Hem*

MACHINE SET-UP: drop upper looper; attach flat sewing surface; etc. see instructional manual for specifics

THREAD: 2-3 cover hem needles: thread to coordinate

cover hem/chain looper: decorative thread – see thread charts on pgs. 30 and 31 for threads that work best

KNIFE/CUTTER: disengaged/non-cutting

DIFFERENTIAL FEED: 1 or "N"; normal

ATTACHMENTS: possible clear cover hem foot or regular foot

TENSIONS: adjust to get "normal" LOOK cover hem stitch

LENGTH: 2 to 4, depending on weight of decorative threads and desired effect

OTHER INSTRUCTIONS: stitch from the wrong side of the fabric

SERGER SET-UP: *2 or 3-Thread Flatlock*

MACHINE SET-UP: wide stitch plate/finger/foot; 2-thread converter on upper looper, if using 2-thread flatlock

THREAD: left* overlock needle: thread to coordinate

upper looper: decorative thread, if using 3-thread; no thread, using 2-thread

lower looper: decorative thread, if using 2-thread; coordinating thread if using 3-thread

KNIFE/CUTTER: disengaged/non-cutting

DIFFERENTIAL FEED: 1 or "N"; normal

ATTACHMENTS: blind hem foot or regular foot

TENSIONS: flatlock LOOK

LENGTH: 1 to 3, depending on weight of decorative threads and desired effect

OTHER INSTRUCTIONS: fold the fabric wrong side together; serge along fabric fold letting enough looper threads hang off the edge for the fabric to lay flat; the use of a blind hem foot on some sergers will help guide the folded edge evenly, adjust as needed. Pull open and press from the wrong side when completed.

*Some 4-thread sergers will only do 3-thread with the right needle. Consult manual or local dealer if needed.

SERGER SET-UP:	*2 or 3-Thread Reverse Flatlock*

MACHINE SET-UP: wide stitch finger/plate/foot; 2-thread converter on upper looper, if using 2-thread flatlock; size 80/12 needle or 90 Topstitch needle

THREAD: left* overlock needle: decorative thread

upper looper: serger thread, if using 3-thread; no thread, using 2-thread

lower looper: serger thread, if using 2-thread; coordinating thread if using 3-thread

KNIFE/CUTTER: disengaged/non-cutting

DIFFERENTIAL FEED: 1 or "N"; normal

ATTACHMENTS: blind hem foot or regular foot

TENSIONS: flatlock LOOK

LENGTH: 1 to 4, depending on weight of decorative threads and desired effect

OTHER INSTRUCTIONS: fold fabric right sides together, serge along fabric fold letting enough looper threads hang off the edge for the fabric to lay flat; the use of a blind hem foot on some sergers will help guide the folded edge evenly, adjust as needed. Pull open and press from the wrong side when completed. Weave other threads under the "bars" if desired. See Novelty Reverse Flatlock for specific weaving ideas.

*Some 4-thread sergers will only do 3-thread with the right overlock needle. Consult manual or local dealer if needed.

5. Position pattern piece on the newly created fabric. Drop seam sealant along the edge of the pattern wherever there is decorative stitching. Allow to dry completely. Cut out piece and construct as pattern indicates.

Kite Tails

Kite Tails is a technique where reversible, decoratively serged, squares are attached to a foundation fabric with a decorative serged rolled hem chain. The end result reminds me of the fabric ties we used to put on our kites as tails.

SERGER SET-UP:	*3-Thread Decorative Edge*
MACHINE SET-UP:	right or left overlock needle; medium width stitch finger(s)/plate; adjust fixed cutter so the fabric does not roll under on the edge
THREAD:	overlock needle: serger thread to coordinate
	upper looper: light to medium weight decorative thread
	lower looper: light to medium weight decorative thread
KNIFE/CUTTER:	engaged/cutting
DIFFERENTIAL FEED:	1 or "N" ; normal
ATTACHMENTS:	none
TENSIONS:	normal balanced 3-thread
LENGTH:	1.5 to 2.5, depending on weight of decorative threads and desired effect; do not shorten too close or it will be more difficult to turn the corner smoothly

SUPPLIES

- fabric(s) for kites
- base project fabric
- 2 spools of light weight and/or medium weight decorative threads (may need an additional spool of medium weight decorative thread)
- 1 spool of thread to coordinate with fabric/decorative threads
- 1 spool of *Woolly Nylon* to coordinate with decorative thread
- glasshead pins
- rotary cutter, mat, ruler
- invisible thread
- size 80/12 Universal needle
- sewing machine
- machine braiding foot

*Design Note: You can use one fabric or several different fabrics.

FABRIC PREPARATION

1. Preshrink, dry and press all fabrics.
2. Cut kite fabrics into 2" squares, using a rotary cutter. Cut twice as many squares as kite tails needed.

1. Place two squares of fabric **wrong** sides together, edges even.

2. Serge around the four sides of the square, turning corners (see instructions on "Turning an Outside Corner" at the end of these instructions). The side of the square that you will want to see on the project should be on top when serging. Leave at least a 1½" thread tail attached to the square.

SERGER SET-UP:	*3-Thread Rolled Hem*
MACHINE SET-UP:	narrow plate/stitch finger/foot; adjust fixed cutter if needed
THREAD:	right* overlock needle: thread to coordinate
	upper looper: medium decorative thread
	lower looper: *Woolly Nylon* to match the decorative thread
KNIFE/CUTTER:	disengaged/non-cutting
DIFFERENTIAL FEED:	1 or "N"
ATTACHMENTS:	none
TENSIONS:	rolled hem
LENGTH:	1.5 to 2; depends on the decorative thread chosen

*There are models of sergers that require the use of the left overlock needle for a rolled hem, not the right. If you have any questions consult your instruction manual (see: rolled hem) or your local dealer.

3. Set up the serger for a 3-thread rolled hem as specified above. Test sew on fabric scraps.

4. Serge off as much yardage of the decorative chain as needed. Hold the chain taut and to the left as it feeds off stitch finger. NOTE: It is easier to create a smooth chain on some machines by taking off the presser foot.

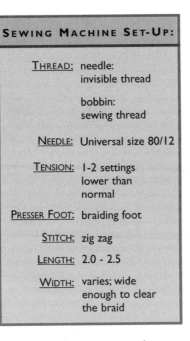

5. OPTIONAL: Position stabilizer under base fabric, if needed.

6. Pin the serged squares in the desired positions on the right side of your project. Tuck the tail under to the wrong side so it will be caught when the squares are sewn in place.

SEWING MACHINE SET-UP:

THREAD:	needle: invisible thread
	bobbin: sewing thread
NEEDLE:	Universal size 80/12
TENSION:	1-2 settings lower than normal
PRESSER FOOT:	braiding foot
STITCH:	zig zag
LENGTH:	2.0 - 2.5
WIDTH:	varies; wide enough to clear the braid

7. Set up the sewing machine as specified above.

8. Thread the decorative chain through the hole of a machine braiding foot. Attach the foot to the machine. Use needle down feature if available.

9. Sew the decorative chain in a random or designed pattern onto the project. As you sew, catch the squares in place by sewing across them diagonally from corner to corner.

Turning an Outside Corner

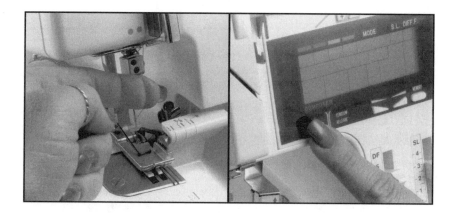 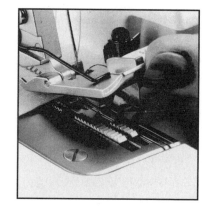 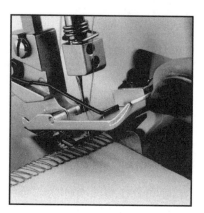

1. Serge slowly to the end of the fabric. Stop with the needle out of the fabric.

2. Gently pull the needle thread right above the needle eye or use a needle tension release button. (There are sergers that disengage the tensions when the presser foot is lifted.) Do not pull out a lot of thread, just release the tautness.

3. While releasing the tension, lift the presser foot and gently pull the thread off the stitch finger and turn the fabric. Be careful not to pull too much chain out or there will be loops in the corner.

Note: Photo shows hand holding foot up to allow you to see under foot. You do not need to hold foot up as shown.

4. Lower the needle using the hand wheel. Align the outside edge of the fabric against the front of the needle and the other side of the corner against the moveable cutter.

5. Lower the presser foot. Pull up on the needle and both looper threads to remove excess slack. Serge.

Note: The corner should look like it has been double stitched.

Rolled Hem Pintucks

A rolled hem leaves a hard edge that looks similar on the front and back. When stitched on a fold, you get pintucks. They stand up nicely and add a little dimension.

SUPPLIES

- fabric (works best with woven fabrics)
- 1 spool of light or medium weight decorative thread
- 1-2 spools of thread to coordinate
- pressing equipment
- serger seam guide or blind hem foot
- glasshead straight pins
- washout pencil or soapstone marker

FABRIC PREPARATION

1. Preshrink, dry and press all fabrics.

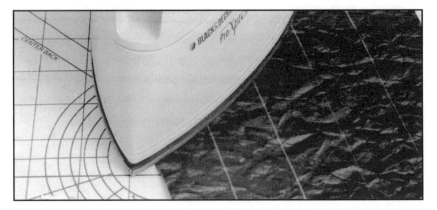

2. Using a soapstone marker, or washout pencil, mark the tuck positions on the right side of the fabric.

3. Fold fabric on tuck line and press.

2 or 3-Thread Rolled Hem

MACHINE SET-UP: narrow stitch plate/finger/foot; 2-thread converter (if using 2-thread rolled hem) on upper looper

THREAD: right* overlock needle: thread to coordinate

upper looper: light or medium weight decorative thread if using 3-thread; no thread for 2-thread

lower looper: thread to coordinate for 3-thread; light or medium weight decorative thread, if using 2-thread

KNIFE/CUTTER: disengaged/non-cutting

DIFFERENTIAL FEED: 1 or "N" ; normal

ATTACHMENTS: blind hem foot or seam guide

TENSIONS: rolled hem/edge

LENGTH: 1.0 to 2.0 depending on the thread and desired results

*There are a few models that require the use of the left overlock needle for a rolled hem, not the right. If you have any questions consult your instruction manual (see: rolled hem) or your local dealer.

1. Set blind hem foot so the guide is just to the right of the needle. If using a seam guide, adjust for the same distance.

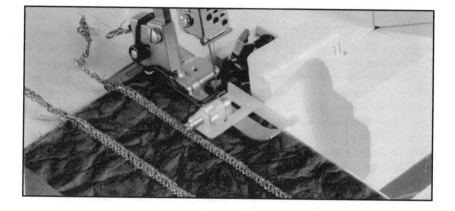

2. Serge the tuck, aligning the fold with the guide on the blind hem foot or seam guide.

Serging Tip: A rolled hem stitch appears different from the top and the underside. To keep the appearance of all tucks the same, always serge with the side of the folded fabric up that you want to be the right side of the tuck. If your design plan requires tucks pressed in two different directions (example: away from center), you will need to serge the tucks from two different directions (top to bottom and bottom to top).

3. Press the tuck in one direction, using a press cloth to protect the decorative thread.

4. Repeat steps 2-3 for each tuck desired.

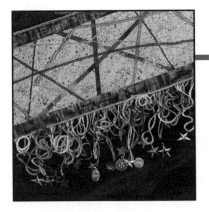

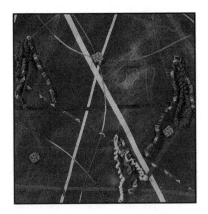

Trims

So many people think sergers are just for seams and seam finishing, but a serger can be a very creative machine, if you just know how.

We have all experienced the need for coordinating trim, (piping/braid, etc.) but either couldn't find the right one, or were sewing at a time when the "all-night sewing store" was not open. The best way to get just the trim to match your project is to create your own!

The following sections are full of all sorts of braids and cords to add surface detail and texture to your projects.

Middy Braid

Middy Braid, or cording, is flat braid that is applied with the sewing machine. It differs from a soutache, or rat tail braid, because it has no filler cord.

SUPPLIES

- 1 spool of decorative thread
- 1 spool of thread to coordinate
- 1 spool of *Woolly Nylon*
- sewing machine
- size 80/12 Universal needle
- invisible thread (optional)
- glasshead pins
- washout pencil

Design Tip: By using *Woolly Nylon Extra* you can make your braid thicker.

SERGER SET-UP:	*3-Thread Rolled Hem*
MACHINE SET-UP:	narrow plate/stitch finger/foot
THREAD:	right* overlock needle: thread to match fabric or to coordinate with decorative thread
	upper looper: medium weight or heavy decorative thread
	lower looper: Woolly Nylon to match or blend with other threads
KNIFE/CUTTER:	disengaged/non-cutting
DIFFERENTIAL FEED:	1 or "N"
ATTACHMENTS:	none
TENSIONS:	rolled hem
LENGTH:	1.5 to 2, depends on the decorative thread chosen
FABRIC	none

*There are a models of that require the use of the left overlock needle for a rolled hem, not the right. If you have any questions consult your instruction manual (see: rolled hem) or your local dealer.

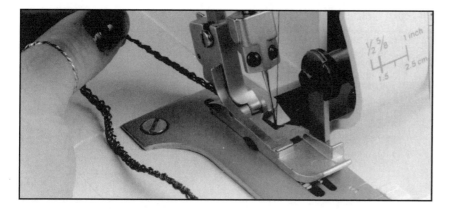

1. First set tensions on fabric, then serge without fabric. As the serger creates the decorative chain, hold the chain taut so that it feeds off the stitch finger to the back of the presser foot. Serge desired amount of decorative chain. NOTE: It is easier to create a smooth chain on some machines by taking the presser foot off.

Serging Tip: If the decorative chain is curling when feeding off or is too curly when removed, loosen the lower looper (*Woolly Nylon*) slightly.

SEWING MACHINE SET-UP:	
THREAD:	needle: invisible thread
	bobbin: sewing thread
NEEDLE:	Universal size 80/12
TENSION:	1-2 settings lower than normal
PRESSER FOOT:	braiding foot
STITCH:	zig zag
LENGTH:	2.0 - 2.5
WIDTH:	varies; wide enough to clear the braid

2. To apply the middy braid to your project, set up the sewing machine as specified above.

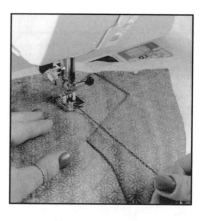

3. Thread the novelty chain through the hole of a braiding foot. Attach the foot to the machine. Use the needle down feature if available.

4. Draw the desired design using a washout pencil. Stitch over the drawn design, holding the chain on top of the design. Straighten braid in front of foot, if needed.

Design Tip: I find quilt templates an excellent source for designs.

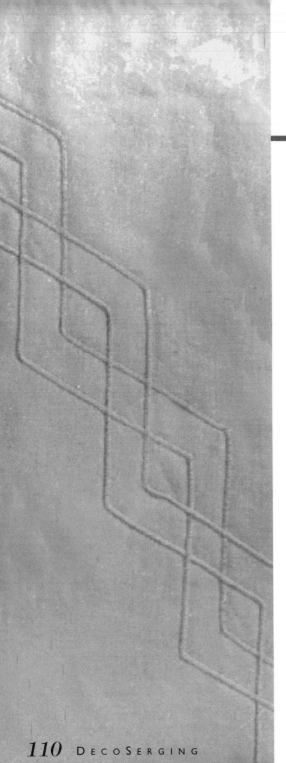

Soutache

Soutache (also known as rat tail braid) is a small round trim created here by serging over a small cord using a decorative rolled hem.

SUPPLIES:

- 1 spool of decorative thread
- 1 spool of thread to coordinate
- *Woolly Nylon* to match decorative thread
- filler cord: *Speed Cro-Sheen, Luster Sheen* or *Pearl Cotton*
- sewing machine
- invisible thread (optional)
- size 80/12 Universal needle
- stabilizer
- washout pencil

SERGER SET-UP:	*3-Thread Rolled Hem*
MACHINE SET-UP:	narrow plate/stitch finger/foot
THREAD:	right* needle: thread to match decorative thread
	upper looper: decorative thread
	lower looper: Woolly Nylon to match or blend with other threads
KNIFE/CUTTER:	disengaged/non-cutting
DIFFERENTIAL FEED:	1 or "N"
ATTACHMENTS:	none
TENSIONS:	rolled hem
LENGTH:	1.5 to 2; depends on the decorative thread chosen

*There are a models that require the use of the left overlock needle for a rolled hem, not the right. If you have any questions consult your instruction manual (see: rolled hem) or your local dealer.

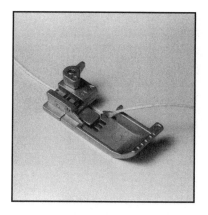

1. Feed the filler cord in the hole of your presser foot.**

** Not all serger brands include a presser foot with a cording hole. Some brands offer an optional accessory for this. When selecting a guiding hole in the presser foot, be certain the hole guides the cord over the rolled hem stitch finger. Consult your instruction manual, work book, or local dealer. This hole is not absolutely necessary but it is very helpful for guiding the cord while sewing.

2. Serge. The rolled hem will cover the cord as you serge. As the serger creates the braid, hold the chain taut as it feeds off the stitch finger. Keep an even speed as you run the serger, feeding the soutache out the back. Serge desired amount of soutache.

SEWING MACHINE SET-UP:	
THREAD:	needle: invisible thread
	bobbin: sewing thread
NEEDLE:	Universal size 80/12
TENSION:	1-2 settings lower than normal
PRESSER FOOT:	braiding foot
STITCH:	zig zag
LENGTH:	2.0 - 2.5
WIDTH:	varies; wide enough to clear the braid

3. Set up the sewing machine as specified above.

4. Thread the novelty chain through the hole of a braiding foot. Attach the foot to the machine. Use needle down feature, if available.

5. Draw the desired design, using a washout pencil on the right sides. Place stabilizer under project fabric.

6. Stitch over the drawn design using the rolled hem chain as a braid in the braiding foot. The braiding foot will control the cord as you sew, but you may need to straighten the cord in front of the foot.

Tassels

Tassels have so many uses for both garments and home decorating. Your serger can help you create one or many in just the right color combinations, even using the same threads you used for other decorative serging on your project.

Tassels can be created using the 3-thread rolled hem chain or the decorative chainstitch. The rolled hem makes a thicker chain, while the chainstitch makes a tight thin chain. Instructions are given for both.

SUPPLIES:

- 1 spool of light or medium weight decorative thread
- 1 spool of *Woolly Nylon* to coordinate with decorative thread, if using 3-thread rolled hem
- 1 spool of thread to coordinate, if using chain stitch instructions
- tassel template, see instructions for description
- seam sealant (*Fray Stop, No Fray, Fray Check*)
- adhesive tape

SERGER SET-UP:	3-Thread Rolled Hem
MACHINE SET-UP:	narrow plate/stitch finger/foot
THREAD:	right* overlock needle: thread to match the fabric or coordinate with decorative thread
	upper looper: medium weight decorative thread
	lower looper: *Woolly Nylon* to coordinate
KNIFE/CUTTER:	disengaged/non-cutting
DIFFERENTIAL FEED:	1 or "N"
ATTACHMENTS:	none
TENSIONS:	rolled hem
LENGTH:	1.5 to 2; depends on the decorative thread used

*There are a few models that require the use of the left overlock needle for a rolled hem, not the right. If you have any questions, consult your instruction manual. (See: rolled hem) or your local dealer.

> **Design Tip:** By using *Woolly Nylon Extra,* the rolled hem chain will be thicker, thus making your tassel fuller.

SERGER SET-UP:	*Decorative Chain Stitch*

MACHINE SET-UP:	as manufacturer instructs for chain stitching
THREAD:	chain needle: regular thread or embroidery thread to coordinate with looper thread
	chain looper: light or medium weight decorative thread
KNIFE/CUTTER:	disengaged/non-cutting
DIFFERENTIAL FEED:	1 or "N"
ATTACHMENTS:	none
TENSIONS:	normal stitch "LOOK"; may need to loosen the chain looper to accommodate for decorative thread
LENGTH:	2.0 to 3.0

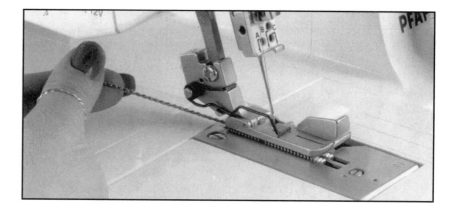

1. First set tensions on fabric, then serge without fabric. As the serger creates the decorative chain, hold the chain taut so that it feeds off the stitch finger (rolled hem) or from under the presser foot. Serge desired amount of decorative chain. NOTE: It is easier to create a smooth rolled hem chain on some machines by taking off the presser foot. It will usually take 6-8 yards of decorative chain for each tassel needed. The more chain, the fuller, or longer, the tassel.

Serging Tip: If the decorative chain is curling when feeding off or is too curly when removed, loosen the lower looper (*Woolly Nylon*) slightly.

 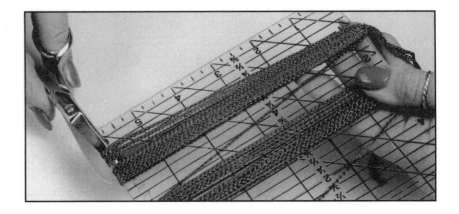

2. Wrap the decorative chain around a tassel template. Anything firm enough (ruler, cardboard) to wrap a lot of chain around can serve as a template. The width of the template determines the length of the tassel. Secure the ends of the chain to the template with tape.

3. Run seam sealant along one end of the chain template and across the decorative chain, as well as on the two ends of the chain. Let the seam sealant dry completely.

4. Take some decorative thread, or more decorative chain, and tie groups of chains together along the non-sealant edge of the template. The quantity depends on thickness of tassel desired; use at least 7-10 chains in each group. Leave a long enough tail on this thread, since it will become the attachment thread.

5. Remove the tassel chains from the template by cutting through the hardened seam sealant.

6. Form the "neck" of the tassel by wrapping decorative thread or chain around the tassel ¼" or more from the top, tied point. Secure the ends within the tassel and add a drop of seam sealant on the knot.

Button Ties

The use of decorative chain to attach buttons to your garment is a creative alternative to sewing them on. It also adds detail and dimension to an otherwise uninspiring part of the garment. These chains can be used to tie on charms as well.

SUPPLIES

- 1 spool of medium weight decorative thread
- 1 spool of thread to coordinate
- 1 spool of *Woolly Nylon* to coordinate
- buttons, or charms with holes
- seam sealant
- sewing machine
- floss threader
- ruler

SERGER SET-UP:	*3-Thread Rolled Hem*
MACHINE SET-UP:	narrow plate/stitch finger/foot
THREAD:	right* overlock needle: thread to match fabric or coordinate with decorative thread
	upper looper: medium weight decorative thread
	lower looper: *Woolly Nylon*
KNIFE/CUTTER:	disengaged/non-cutting
DIFFERENTIAL FEED:	1 or "N"
ATTACHMENTS:	none
TENSIONS:	rolled hem
LENGTH:	1.5 to 2; depends on the decorative thread chosen

*There are models that require the use of the left overlock needle for a rolled hem, not the right. If you have any questions consult your instruction manual (see: rolled hem) or your local dealer.

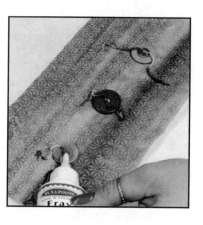

1. After setting the tensions, serge. As the serger creates the decorative chain, hold the chain taut as it feeds off the stitch finger to the back of the presser foot. Serge the desired amount of decorative chain. NOTE: It is easier to create a smooth chain on some machines by taking the presser foot off.

2. Measure and apply seam sealant every 4-6" along the decorative chain. Let dry. Cut the chain into the premeasured lengths through the hardened seam sealant. The longer the lengths, the longer the ties will hang down from the button. You will need 1-2 strands of decorative chain per set of holes in the button or charm.

> **Serging Tip: If the decorative chain is curling when feeding off or is too curly when removed, loosen the lower looper (*Woolly Nylon*) slightly.**

3. Set up the sewing machine as specified above. Use needle down feature if available.

4. Set the button ties in place on the project where the button position is to be. Secure by straight stitching back and forth, in the center, perpendicular to the ties.

5. Thread the decorative chain through the hole(s) on the button or charm with the help of a floss threader. Tie the chains in a knot on top of the button to secure. Place a few drops of seam sealant on the knot to keep it tied. If the chain ends become frayed from threading through button holes, reapply seam sealant, allow to dry, and trim smoothly.

Chapter 23

Charming Chains

This technique uses a rolled hem chain serged over fishing line to hold all sorts of charms and shank buttons. Charming Chains can be used as a trim and applied as a braid, enclosed in a seam as fringe, or used to make jewelry.

SUPPLIES

- I spool of light or medium weight decorative thread
- I spool of *Woolly Nylon,* to coordinate with decorative thread (optional)
- I spool of thread to coordinate
- novelty charms or buttons with a shank
- 10-20 lb. test clear fishing line
- invisible thread
- sewing machine
- size 80/12 Universal needle

SERGER SET-UP:	*3-Thread Rolled Hem*
MACHINE SET-UP:	narrow plate/stitch finger/foot
THREAD:	right* overlock needle: thread to match decorative thread
	upper looper: decorative thread
	lower looper: coordinating thread or *Woolly Nylon* to match decorative thread
KNIFE/CUTTER:	disengaged/non-cutting
DIFFERENTIAL FEED:	1 or "N"
ATTACHMENTS:	none
TENSIONS:	rolled hem
LENGTH:	1.5 to 2; depends on the decorative thread chosen

*There are a few models that require the use of the left overlock needle for a rolled hem, not the right. If you have any questions consult your instruction manual (see: rolled hem) or your local dealer.

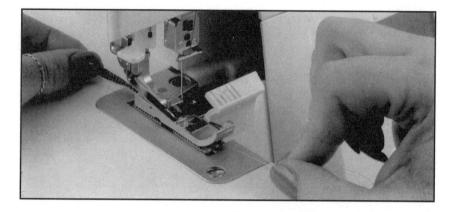 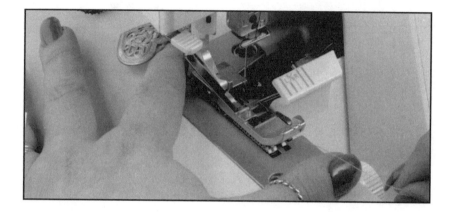

1. Cut a piece of fishing line at least 15" longer than finished desired length.

2. Lift up the serger presser foot and slip the fishing line under, holding 5-6" of loose fishing line behind the presser foot. The line should lay over the stitch finger. Serge 5-6" catching it in the rolled hem being formed over the stitch finger. Hold the fishing line tail taut to keep it and the chain feeding freely from under the presser foot.

3. Slip a charm onto the unserged or front end of the fishing line.

4. Raise the presser foot and slide the charm and excess fishing line behind the presser foot. Slip the loose fishing line back over the stitch finger and lower the presser foot. Hold the charm, excess fishing line and chain behind the presser foot and serge. Continue serging until you reach the point where you want another charm.

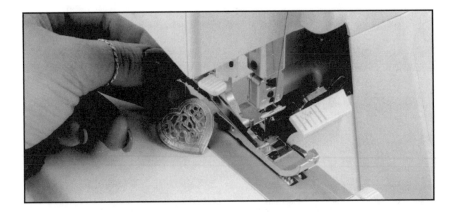

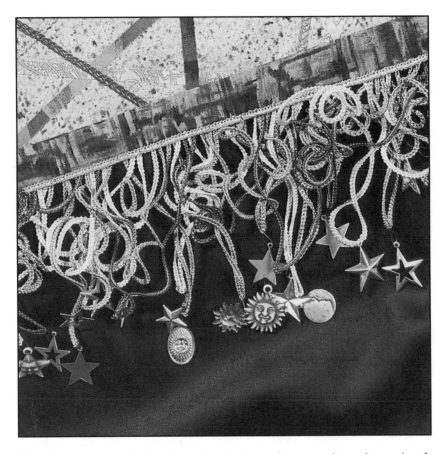

5. Pull on the end of the fishing line, in front of the foot, and remove any excess fishing line at the previous charm. The charm should now lay snug against the chain.

6. Repeat steps 3, 4 and 5 until the charming chain is complete.

There are many uses for charming chains such as: catching the ends of shorter lengths into a seam to create a novelty fringe (pictured above). They could be grouped together and finished with jewelry findings for a necklace or bracelet. Or use them as a novelty braid and couch them on the fabric surface using a sewing machine.

Following are instructions on how to couch charming chains to a fabric surface.

1. Set the sewing machine as specified above.

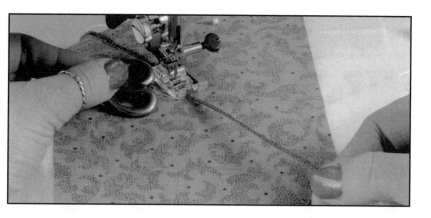

2. Zig zag over the chain. As you come to the charm, pull it and some excess fishing line out and behind the presser foot (similar to creating the trim on the serger). Continue sewing past the charm.

3. After stitching past the charm area, pull the excess fishing line smooth again so the charm will lay smoothly against the braid.

Design Tip: If you need to remove a charm that was serged in the wrong spot, simply cut the fishing line and slip it off. Pull up any excess fishing line that shows.

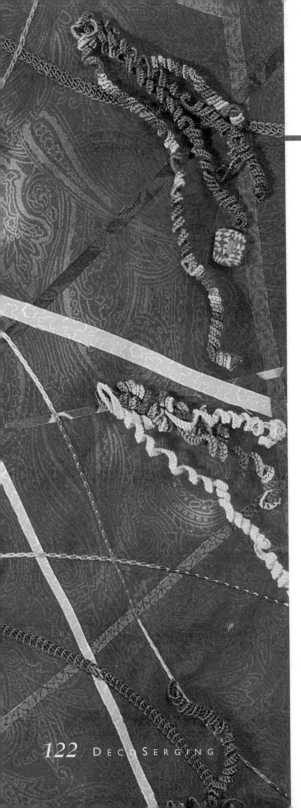

Curly Ringlets

Curly ringlets are a fun technique to add texture to a project. They curl tight and remind me of Shirley Temple's hair ringlets.

SUPPLIES

- 1 spool of medium weight decorative thread
- 1 spool of *Woolly Nylon* to coordinate with decorative thread
- 1 cone thread to coordinate
- ruler
- sewing machine
- seam sealant
  (Fray Check, No Fray, Fray Stop)

SERGER SET-UP:	*3-Thread Rolled Hem*
MACHINE SET-UP:	narrow plate/stitch finger/foot
THREAD:	right* overlock needle: thread to match decorative thread
	upper looper: decorative thread
	lower looper: *Woolly Nylon* to match decorative thread
KNIFE/CUTTER:	disengaged/non-cutting
DIFFERENTIAL FEED:	1 or "N"
ATTACHMENTS:	none
TENSIONS:	rolled hem
LENGTH:	1.5 to 2; depends on the decorative thread chosen

*There are a few models that require the use of the left overlock needle for a rolled hem, not the right. If you have any questions consult your instruction manual (see: rolled hem) or your local dealer.

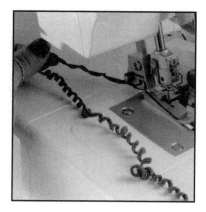

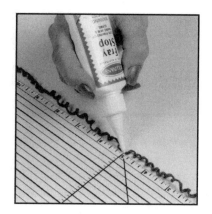

SEWING MACHINE SET-UP:	
THREAD:	needle: sewing or cone thread
	bobbin: sewing thread
NEEDLE:	as needed for project
TENSION:	normal
PRESSER FOOT:	embroidery
STITCH:	straight stitch
LENGTH:	0.5 to 1.0
WIDTH:	0

1. Tighten the tension on the *Woolly Nylon* by 1-2 settings (if possible) higher than needed for a fabric rolled hem.

2. Serge. As the serger creates a decorative chain, hold the chain taut as it feeds off the stitch finger to the back of the foot. NOTE: This chain will feel tight and tend to curl, which is what you want. It is easier to create a smooth chain on some machines by taking the presser foot off.

3. Decide approximately how long you want each Curly Ringlet to be and how many you want. Serge twice this length.

4. Using a ruler, measure twice the desired length, along the chain. Drop seam sealant at this measure point. Allow it to dry completely.

5. Cut the chain in the middle of the dried seam sealant, which should be hard. If the chain starts to unravel, apply more seam sealant; allow to dry and trim smooth.

6. Set up the sewing machine as specified above.

7. Divide the short chains into groups of 3 or more (quantity as desired). Position the group on your project. Secure by straight stitching back and forth, in the center, perpendicular to the ties.

Design Idea: These can also be caught in a seam for a curly type of fringe.

Piping

Piping is a very professional addition to a seam. But as with braids, you cannot always find just what you need, so why not create your own!

SUPPLIES

- 1 spool of decorative thread
- 1 spool of thread to coordinate
- *Woolly Nylon* to match decorative thread
- 1¼" *Seams Great* or 1¼" bias cut tricot interfacing
- filler cord, use *Speed Cro-Sheen* or *Pearl Cotton*
- sewing machine
- glasshead pins
- serger blind hem or cording foot (see note with step 2)

SERGER SET-UP:	*3-Thread Rolled Hem*
MACHINE SET-UP:	narrow plate/stitch finger/foot
THREAD:	right* needle: serger thread to match fabric
	upper looper: decorative thread
	lower looper: *Woolly Nylon* to match fabric
KNIFE/CUTTER:	disengaged/non-cutting
DIFFERENTIAL FEED:	1 or "N"
ATTACHMENTS:	blind hem or cording foot
TENSIONS:	rolled hem
LENGTH:	1.5 to 2, depending on the decorative thread

*There are models that require the use of the left overlock needle for a rolled hem, not the right. If you have any questions consult your instruction manual (see: rolled hem) or your local dealer.

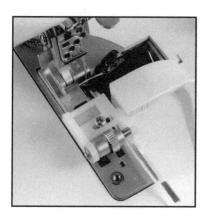

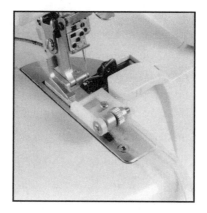

1. Adjust and set tensions on scrap fabric, then serge over filler cord to test.

2. Slide filler cord under the blind hem foot, and adjust the guide so the cord is sandwiched between the needle and the guide. Serge over filler cord 2-3" to anchor the cord to the serger.

3. Fold *Seams Great* or tricot around the cording, raw edges to the left. NOTE: the tricot will curl towards the right side; do not fight the curl when wrapping the tricot around the cord.

4. Serge over the tricot covered cord, being careful not to sew through the cord. You are encasing the tricot covered cord with the rolled hem.

5. The excess *Seams Great* or tricot, becomes the seam allowance for the piping. Insert piping into a seam using the machine and/or serger with a piping/cording or zipper foot.

Sergers with blind hem feet that do not have adjustable guides, or only work with the left serger needle, will not be usable for this technique. If you can not use the blind hem foot, you will need to manually guide everything. Some sergers have a cording foot that can be used to guide the filler cord and bias tricot.

Wide Overlock Braid

Making braids with your serger will guarantee that you will achieve that special look you are striving for. Get extra creative and blend two or more threads together and create a really unique, one-of-a-kind braid.

Wide Braid is a basic braid created with a serger and then applied with a sewing machine.

SUPPLIES

- 1 spool of decorative thread
- 2 spools of thread to coordinate
- 1¼" wide *Seams Great* or 1¼" bias cut tricot interfacing
- sewing machine
- invisible thread (optional)
- size 80/12 Universal needle
- glasshead pins
- washout pencil or soapstone
- stabilizer

SERGER SET-UP:	*Wide 3-Thread Overlock*
MACHINE SET-UP:	wide plate/stitch finger/foot
THREAD:	left* overlock needle: thread to coordinate with decorative thread
	upper looper: decorative thread
	lower looper: serger thread to coordinate with decorative thread**
KNIFE/CUTTER:	engaged/cutting
DIFFERENTIAL FEED:	1 or "N"
ATTACHMENTS:	none
TENSIONS:	normal/balanced 3-thread wide
LENGTH:	varies—depends on weight/thickness of decorative thread; do not use too short of length or the thread will pile up, jam, or not look smooth

*There are models that require the use of only the right needle for a 3-thread overlock, not the left. If you have any questions consult your instruction manual or your local dealer.

DESIGN IDEA: To make a fusible braid, thread the lower looper with a heat adhesive thread, like Threadfuse or Stitch & Fuse. Adjust the tensions to roll slightly to the back, so the adhesive does not show on the front.

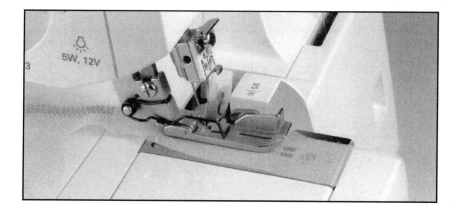

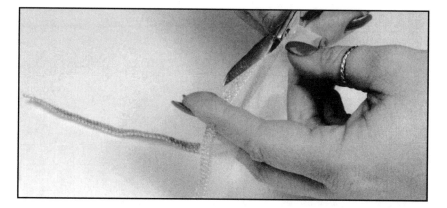

1. Test tensions on scrap fabric first, then test on *Seams Great.*

2. Serge over the 1¼" *Seams Great* as follows: lay the *Seams Great* under the serger presser foot so the tricot seam binding curls under or away from you. Feed the tricot so the cutter just skims the edge off as you serge. NOTE: If stitches don't form consistently, use two layers of *Seams Great.*

3. Trim off the excess tricot carefully from the other side of the trim. Be careful not to stretch the tricot as you trim.

4. If necessary, press the braid smooth with an iron, on a setting no hotter than "wool".

Wide Overlock Braid *(cont.)*

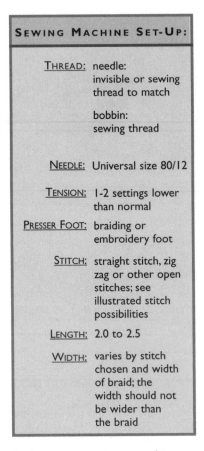

SEWING MACHINE SET-UP:

THREAD: needle:
invisible or sewing
thread to match

bobbin:
sewing thread

NEEDLE: Universal size 80/12

TENSION: 1-2 settings lower
than normal

PRESSER FOOT: braiding or
embroidery foot

STITCH: straight stitch, zig
zag or other open
stitches; see
illustrated stitch
possibilities

LENGTH: 2.0 to 2.5

WIDTH: varies by stitch
chosen and width
of braid; the
width should not
be wider than
the braid

5. Set up sewing machine as specified above. Use needle down feature if available.

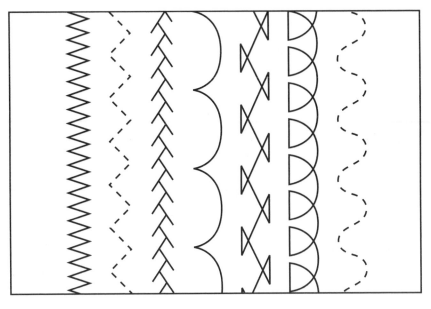

Machine stitch possibilities for sewing on braid.

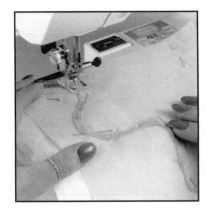

6. Use a washout pencil to draw your design on the right side of the project fabric. Place stabilizer under project fabric. Pin in place if needed.

7. Sew the braid onto the project following design lines. Use the needle down feature if available. If your design is more intricate, you may want to pin the braid in position before sewing.

Reversible Overlock Braid

This is a unique variation of the regular wide braid created by stitching with a different decorative thread in each looper. As you apply this braid, you flip it over to reveal the other color and add the texture of the twist.

SUPPLIES:

- 2 spools of coordinating decorative thread
- 1 spool of thread to coordinate
- 1¼" *Seams Great* or 1¼" bias cut tricot interfacing
- sewing machine
- invisible thread (optional)
- size 80/12 Universal needle
- glasshead pins
- washout pencil or soapstone
- stabilizer

SERGER SET-UP:	Wide 3-Thread Overlock
MACHINE SET-UP:	wide plate/stitch finger/foot
THREAD:	left* overlock needle: thread to coordinate
	upper looper: decorative thread
	lower looper: thread to coordinate with decorative threads
KNIFE/CUTTER:	engaged/cutting
DIFFERENTIAL FEED:	1 or "N"
ATTACHMENTS:	none
TENSIONS:	normal/balanced 3-thread wide
LENGTH:	varies—depends on weight/thickness of decorative thread; do not use too short of length or the braid will look rough

*There are models that require the use of only the right needle for a 3-thread overlock, not the left. If you have any questions consult your instruction manual or your local dealer.

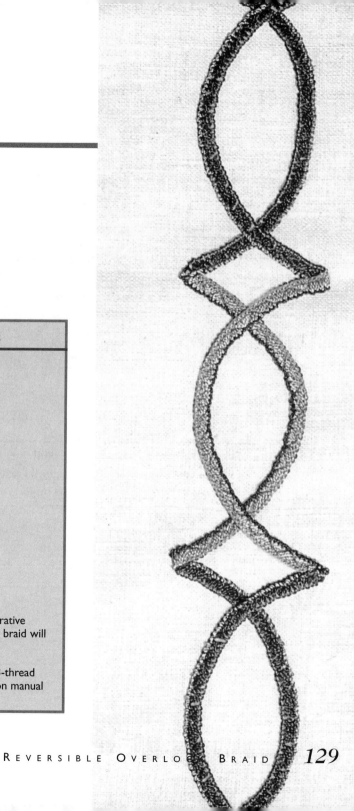

Reversible Overlock Braid *(cont.)*

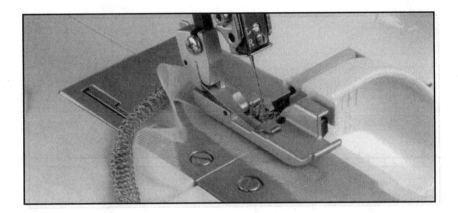

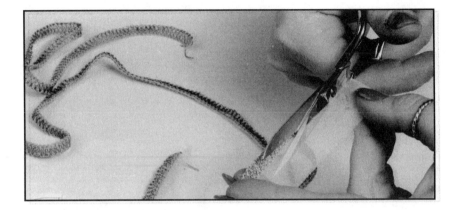

1. Adjust and test tensions on scrap fabric, then test on *Seams Great.*

> **Note: When stretched, *(Seams Great)* will curl to the right side. To prevent the curl from fighting you while stitching, we place the curl rolling under against the feed dogs.**

2. Serge over the 1¼" *Seams Great* as follows: lay the *Seams Great* under the serger presser foot so the tricot seam binding curls under or away from you. Feed the tricot so the cutter just skims the edges off as you serge. NOTE: If stitches don't form consistently, use two layers of *Seams Great.*

3. Trim off the excess tricot carefully from the other side of the trim. Be careful not to stretch the tricot as you trim.

4. If necessary, press the braid smooth with an iron, on a setting no hotter than "wool".

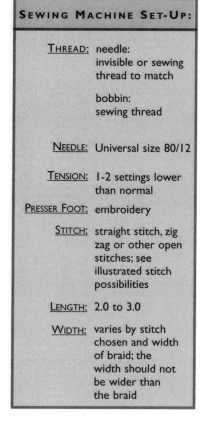

SEWING MACHINE SET-UP:

THREAD: needle: invisible or sewing thread to match

bobbin: sewing thread

NEEDLE: Universal size 80/12

TENSION: 1-2 settings lower than normal

PRESSER FOOT: embroidery

STITCH: straight stitch, zig zag or other open stitches; see illustrated stitch possibilities

LENGTH: 2.0 to 3.0

WIDTH: varies by stitch chosen and width of braid; the width should not be wider than the braid

5. Set up sewing machine as specified above.

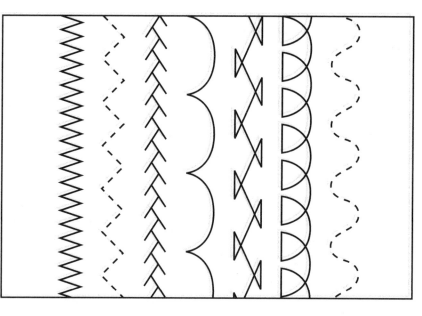

Machine stitch possibilities for sewing on braid.

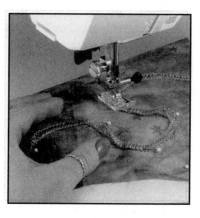

6. Use a washout pencil to draw your design on the right side of the project fabric. Place stabilizer under project fabric if needed.

7. Pin the braid in place as desired. Flip over to expose the different thread on the reverse side. Stitch braid in place, stopping and restarting sewing at flip over points, to allow these areas to add texture. Use needle down feature on machine if it is available.

Cover Hem Braid

The cover hem stitch can be stitched directly onto the fabric, so why make a braid? The end result of the braid and how interesting it looks on the fabric is quite different than stitching it.

Cover hem braid stretches like a knitted braid or cord. The width of the braid varies by the type of cover hem used (wide, narrow or triple). The triple cover hem makes a wider more dense looking braid. The type and weight of the decorative thread used will also effect the thickness.

SUPPLIES

- 1 spool of medium weight decorative thread-see charts, pgs. 30 and 31 for cover hem looper
- 2-3 spools/cones of thread to coordinate
- water soluble stabilizer (*Aqua Solve, Solvy, Wash Away, Avalon*)
- regular stabilizer
- sewing machine
- invisible thread (optional)
- size 80/12 Universal needle
- braiding foot for sewing machine

FABRIC PREPARATION

1. Press four layers of water soluble stabilizer together to create one thick piece. Use a **dry** iron and press on wool setting.
2. Cut water soluble stabilizer into 1" strips.

SERGER SET-UP:	*Cover Hem*
MACHINE SET-UP:	two or three left, cover hem needles*; upper looper disengaged; refer to serger instruction manual for other specifics
THREAD:	2-3 left cover hem needles*: thread to coordinate with decorative thread
	cover hem/chain looper: medium weight decorative thread; see thread chart for cover hem
KNIFE/CUTTER:	disengaged/non-cutting
DIFFERENTIAL FEED:	1 or "N"
ATTACHMENTS:	none
TENSIONS:	normal cover hem, adjust tensions as needed
LENGTH:	1.5 to 2.5; varies by weight/thickness of decorative thread; do not use too short of length or the thread will pile up and jam

*These left needles are different from the overlock left needles. The cover hem feature is available on a few sergers from various machine companies.

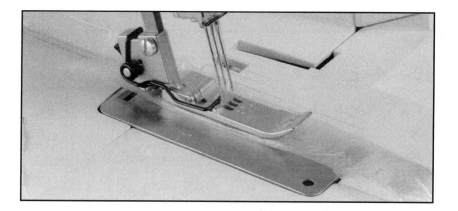

1. Adjust tensions as needed and test sew on a scrap of fabric. Remember this stitch does not chain for very long without fabric, so keep fabric scraps handy, if needed.

2. Serge onto a 1" strip of water soluble stabilizer. As you get to the end of the strip just slip the next four layer strip under the presser foot. The stitching will not look different if the stabilizer overlaps. NOTE: As you stitch, if you look at the back, do not be concerned if it looks like the stitch is more narrow in places. The needles have just split the stabilizer.

3. Rinse or soak the soluble stabilizer off in cool, clear water. **Do not** rush and try to pull away the excess stabilizer because it pulls the needle threads out into loops or breaks them. Allow to dry, or press dry covered with a press cloth. Before pressing, test a small sample to make sure your decorative thread does not melt or shrink up.

SEWING MACHINE SET-UP:

THREAD:	needle: invisible thread
	bobbin: sewing thread
NEEDLE:	1-2 settings lower than normal
TENSION:	Universal size 80/12
PRESSER FOOT:	braiding or embroidery, slip the braid through the slot in the foot
STITCH:	multi-step zig zag
LENGTH:	2.0 to 2.5
WIDTH:	varies by width of braid; the width should not be wider than the braid

4. Set up the sewing machine as specified above.

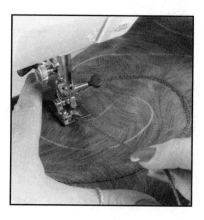

5. Draw your design using a washout pencil.

6. Sew braid onto the project following design lines. Use needle down feature if available. If your design is more intricate, you may want to hand position and pin the braid before sewing. Be careful not to pull the braid as it has some stretch.

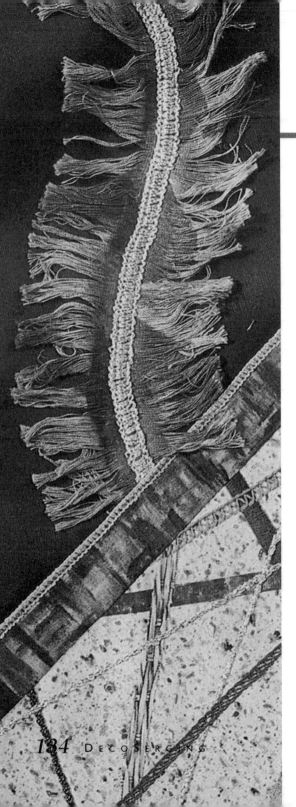

Flatlock Fringe

This technique results in a pseudo braid with an attitude! This trim not only creates a braid, but adds texture with the fringe. The flatlocked narrow strip is raveled out to create the fringe. A fusible thread is used in the needle when flatlocking, to aid in the positioning of the fringe.

SUPPLIES

- woven fabric **only**
- 1 spool of decorative thread
- 1 spool of *Thread Fuse* or *Stitch & Fuse*
- 1 spool of thread to coordinate with fabric/decorative thread
- metallic needle
  (Metallica, Metallic, Metafil, Metalfil)
- glasshead straight pins
- rotary cutter, ruler, mat
- invisible thread
- sewing machine
- size 80/12 Universal needle

FABRIC PREPARATION

1. Preshrink dry and press all fabrics, interfacing.
2. Cut fabric(s) into 2-3" strips, using a rotary cutter, mat, ruler. Strip width can vary as desired, 1½" or wider.

SERGER SET-UP:	2 or 3-Thread Flatlock
MACHINE SET-UP:	left* overlock needle; a wide plate/stitch finger; metallic 80/12 or 90/14 needle
THREAD:	left* overlock needle: Thread Fuse or Stitch & Fuse
	upper looper: decorative thread, if using 3-thread; no thread if using 2-thread
	lower looper: coordinating thread, if using 3-thread; decorative thread, if using 2-thread flatlock
KNIFE/CUTTER:	disengaged/non-cutting
DIFFERENTIAL FEED:	1 or "N"
ATTACHMENTS:	blind hem foot very helpful
TENSIONS:	flatlock
LENGTH:	1-2, depending on weight of decorative threads and desired effect

*Most 4-threads will use the left overlock needle; most 5-thread sergers will use the right (back) needle (if your 5-thread has two right (back) needle positions, use the most outside/left of this needle position). Check your instruction manual, or local dealer, to verify any questions.

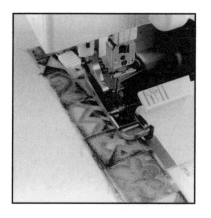

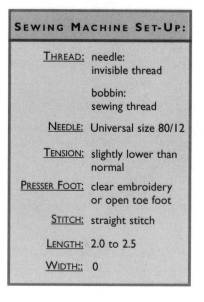

SEWING MACHINE SET-UP:	
THREAD:	needle: invisible thread
	bobbin: sewing thread
NEEDLE:	Universal size 80/12
TENSION:	slightly lower than normal
PRESSER FOOT:	clear embroidery or open toe foot
STITCH:	straight stitch
LENGTH:	2.0 to 2.5
WIDTH::	0

1. Fold the fabric strip in half lengthwise, wrong sides together, and press the fold.

2. Serge along the fold. Allow some of the loops to hang off the folded edge so the flatlock will lay flat when pulled apart. Practice guiding the folded edge through with a fabric scrap. The use of a blind hem foot on some sergers can aid in guiding the fold consistently. Pull the strip flat and finger press.

3. Unravel the fabric edges all the way to the serged center. Clip any threads needed to unravel completely.

4. Position and pin the fringe in place. Press, using a steam iron.

5. Set up the sewing machine as specified above.

6. To permanently hold the fringe, stitch into place along both edges of the flatlock stitch with the sewing machine.

Toggle Buttons

Toggles make an interesting fastening to garments or bags. Or they can be added randomly to projects for dimension. The following section shows two variations of toggle buttons.

SUPPLIES

- fabric (s)
- 1 spool of decorative thread
- 2 spools of thread to
  coordinate with
  fabric/decorative threads
- glasshead straight pins
- glue stick or other fabric glue
- seam sealant
  (Fray Check, No Fray, Fray Stop)
- paper backed fusible webbing
  *(Wonder Under, Aleen's, Stitch
  Witchery Plus, Heat and Bond
  Lite, etc.)*
- rotary cutter, ruler, mat

SERGER SET-UP:	Rolled Hem or Narrow Hem
MACHINE SET-UP:	narrow plate/stitch finger/foot; fixed cutter adjustments as machine manual instructs
THREAD:	right* overlock needle: thread to coordinate
	upper looper: decorative thread
	lower looper: thread to coordinate
KNIFE/CUTTER:	engaged/cutting
DIFFERENTIAL FEED:	1 or "N"
ATTACHMENTS:	none
TENSIONS:	rolled hem or narrow hem as desired
LENGTH:	1.5 to 2; depends on the decorative thread chosen

*There are models that require the use of the left overlock needle for a rolled hem, not the right. If you have any questions consult your instruction manual (see: rolled hem) or your local dealer.

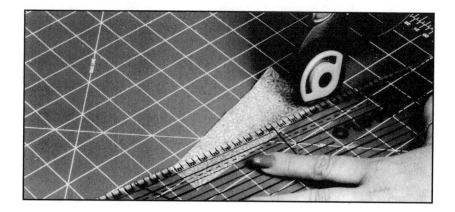

FABRIC PREPARATION

1. Preshrink, dry and press all fabrics.

2. *Cut a strip of fusible webbing a little wider than the desired finished width of the button.

3. *Fuse the webbing across half the width of the fabric (center fold to selvage). Remove the paper backing. Fold the fabric in half, crossgrain matching the selvages; press to fuse.

4. Cut this fused strip of fabric the width of the finished toggle.

5. Cut strip into 8"-12" lengths. You will want to experiment with the length on your first button to find what you like or how thick you want your toggle.

6. OPTIONAL: If you want another shape variation, cut the 8"-12" strips into a wedge or elongated triangle.

---

* Note: if fabric is very thick or firm, eliminate these steps.

Toggle Buttons *(cont.)*

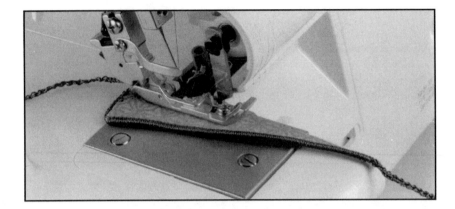

1. For the tube style, serge the two long edges of the strip. For the barrel style, serge from the narrow to the wide end first, then from the wide end to the point. Let the serger trim off the decorative tail from first row of stitching.

2. Secure the tail ends with a seam sealant. Let dry and trim off serged tails.

3. Place a little amount of glue down the center of the wrong side of the toggle strip.

4a. For the barrel style: Start rolling at the widest, unfinished edge and roll to the point. Use a needle, toothpick, or *Tail Tucker,* to roll tightly around. Secure the point with more fabric glue, if needed. Pin end in place until glue dries. Remove the needle, toothpick, or *Tail Tucker.*

4b. For the tube style: Roll the serged strip, from unfinished edge to unfinished edge, tightly around a needle, toothpick, or *Tail Tucker.* Finger press the end to secure and use more fabric glue, if needed. Pin end in place until glue dries. Remove the needle, toothpick, or *Tail Tucker.*

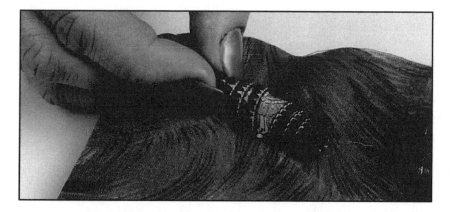

5. By hand, whip stitch the button end in place. Place on project in desired location with point or unfinished edge against fabric. Stitch the button in place, creating a thread shank as you sew.

Design Note: For more novelty toggles you can wrap decorative chain around the toggle and secure the end.

Glossary

blind hem

This is an invisible stitched hem. In this book, we use the blind hem foot as a stitching guide for a number of techniques because it has an adjustable guide.

chain

The loose stitch a serger forms in the air over stitch fingers as the machine runs without fabric. It can consist of 2,3,4, or 5 threads.

chain looper

The looper that forms the underneath, knot-like part of the chain stitch. The looper rotates in an oval manner and usually moves from right to left to connect with a chain stitch needle. Instruction manuals may call this the front looper.

chain stitch

The straight stitch some sergers form using a chain looper and a chain needle.

chaining off

As a serger overlocks, it creates a knitted thread chain with the loopers. The act of sewing without the fabric and letting this form is called chaining off.

differential feed

A two-part feed dog system that has adjustments to run the front feed dogs at different speeds (slower or faster) than the back feed dogs. It is used to compensate for the differences in fabrics (grainline, weight, type) and to aid in more efficiently accomplishing some techniques (gathering).

fixed or stationary cutter/blade

The straight, flat part of the cutter. It appears to be a cut out portion of the plate and is found under the presser foot. The flat portion of the cutting system that the moveable blade presses against. The portion of the cutting system that does not move when the serger is in operation.

fuzzies

These are the fibers that poke out and start to unravel from a cut edge. The serger blade is used to eliminate these.

hiccups

Inconsistent stitches formed due to irregular feeding of the thread(s).

lower looper

The overlock looper that moves from left to right and forms the lower/underside of the stitch. Instruction manuals may call this the bottom looper.

Glossary

movable cutter/blade

One of two parts of the cutting system. The part that moves when the machine runs or the hand wheel is turned. It can hang from the top, or it can look like a question mark (?) and come from under the plate.

overlock needle

The needle used to lock the upper and/or lower looper threads onto the fabric. On most 4 and 5-thread machines there are two overlock needles, left and right. On 5-thread sergers, do not confuse this with your left needle(s); they are for chain stitching and/or cover hem.

rotary cutter

A cutting tool that has a round razor-sharp blade. It is like a pizza cutter for fabrics. The cutter must be used with a specially designed mat to protect the cutting surface from the sharp blade and prevent the blade from getting dull against a hard surface.

stabilizer

This is a product that is used to prevent fabric from puckering up or stretching out of shape while stitching is taking place. Most traditional brands (Stitch and Ditch, Tear Away, Tear Easy, etc.) are placed on the wrong side of the project fabric and removed after the stitching is completed.

stitch finger

The part of the serger over which the overlock stitch forms. It can be found on the plate and/or the presser foot. The width of the stitch finger(s) determines the width of the overlock stitch.

stitch length

This is the distance between each stitch that is formed. The normal setting for most machines is 2.0 - 3.0.

upper looper

The overlock looper that moves from right to left and forms the right side/upper side of the stitch. Instruction manuals may call this the top looper.

Bibliography

Bradkin, Cheryl Greider. Basic Seminole Patchwork.
Mt. View, CA: Leone Publications, 1990.

Brown, Gail and Pati Palmer. Sewing With Sergers.
Portland, OR: Palmer/Pletsch, 1985.

Palmer, Pati and Gail Brown. Creative Serging.
Portland, OR: Palmer/Pletsch, 1987

Palmer, Pati, Gail Brown and Sue Green. The New Creative Serging Illustrated.
Radnor, PA: Chilton Book Company, 1994.

Price, Ann Hesse. The Serger Idea Book.
Portland, OR: Palmer/Pletsch Incorporated, 1989

Young, Tammy and Lori Bottom. ABC's of Serging.
Radnor, PA: Chilton Book Company, 1992.

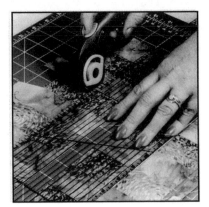

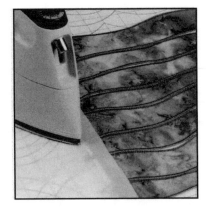

Resources

Baby Lock
1760 Gilsinn Lane
Fenton, MO 63026

Bernina of America
3500 Thayer Court
Aurora, IL 60504

Brother International Corporation
200 Cottontail Lane
Somerset, NJ 08875

Elna, USA
1760 Gilsinn Lane
Fenton, MO 63026

Husqvarna Viking & White
11760 Berea Road
Cleveland, OH 44111

Juki Industries of America
5 Haul Road
Wayne, NJ 07470

June Tailor
2861 Highway 175
Rickfield, WI 53026

New Home Sewing Machine Co.
10 Industrial Avenue
Mahwah, NJ 07430

Pfaff American Sales Corporation
610 Winters Avenue
Paramus, NJ 07653

Riccar
1800 East Walnut Avenue
Fullerton, CA 92831

SCS USA - Madeira
9631 North East Colfax Street
Portland, OR 97220
(888) 623-3472

Singer Sewing Company
4500 Singer Road
Murfreesboro, TN 37130

Sullivans Sewing Notions
5221 Thatcher Road
Downers Grove, IL 60515
(dealers only)

Fiskars Inc.
Box 8027
Wausau, WI 54402

YLI Corporation
161 West Main Street
Rockhill, SC 29730
(800) 296-8139

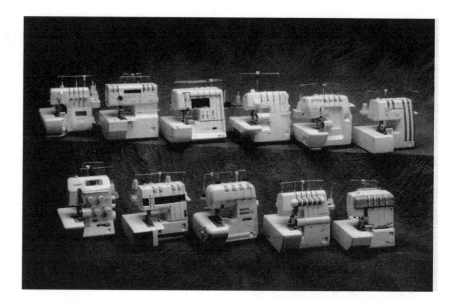

Mail order

Clotilde
(800) 772-2891 for free catalog
notions, threads, books, videos

Nancy's Notions
333 Beichl Avenue
Beaver Dam, WI 53916
(800) 833-0690 for free catalog
notions, threads, books, videos, fabric

Web of Threads
1410 Broadway
Paducah, KY 42001
(800) 955-8185

Arlington Sewing Center
1920 W. Henderson Road
Columbus, OH 43220
(614) 538-8722
(inside Hancock Fabrics)
no catalog
notions, sewing supplies

About the Author

April Dunn was born and raised in St. Louis, Missouri and is a graduate of the University of Missouri-Columbia in Textiles. She is a freelance Sewing Educator that has been Swiss-trained and travels around the world conducting classes and seminars on sewing and serging.

Her credits include:

...contributing designer for *Sew and Serge Terrific Textures* and *A Creative Needle Christmas* books;

...a bi-monthly column in *Creative Needle* titled *Marketplace;*

...articles in *Creative Needle, Serger Update* and *Sew News* magazines;

...articles for trade publications – *Round Bobbin* and *Sewing Professional;*

...writing the decorative thread brochure for YLI;

...two Italian training videos –1996.

She has been an instructor at the following schools:

American Sewing Guild National Convention 1997 – Houston;

Martha Pullen's School of Art Fashion 1989, 1990, 1996;

Rocky Mountain Sewing Festival 1995, 1996;

Sewing at the Ocean 1994 – Melbourne, FL;

Sewing in the Mountains 1990 to 1993 – Maggie Valley, NC ;

Sewing with Elna in the Heartlands 1992 – Columbus, OH;

Sewing with Elna in Olde Sacramento 1991;

Elna Impact 1988 to 1994, 1997.

She has also taught for many dealers, sewing and smocking guilds/clubs.